LINCOLN CHRISTIAN COLLEGE AND SEMINARY

The
Differentiated
Classroom

Responding to the Needs of All Learners

Carol Ann Tomlinson

Association for Supervision and Curriculum Development
Alexandria, VA USA

P9-DDY-844

Association for Supervision and Curriculum Development
1703 N. Beauregard St. • Alexandria, VA 22311-1714 USA
Telephone: 1-800-933-2723 or 703-578-9600 • Fax: 703-575-5400
Web site: http://www.ascd.org • E-mail: member@ascd.org

Gene R. Carter, *Executive Director*
Michelle Terry, *Associate Executive Director, Program Development*
Nancy Modrak, *Director, Publishing*
John O'Neil, *Director of Acquisitions*
Julie Houtz, *Managing Editor of Books*
Darcie Simpson, *Associate Editor*
René Bahrenfuss, *Copy Editor*
Charles D. Halverson, *Project Assistant*
Gary Bloom, *Director, Design and Production Services*
Karen Monaco, *Senior Designer*
Judi Connelly, *Designer*
Tracey A. Smith, *Production Manager*
Dina Murray, *Production Coordinator*
John Franklin, *Production Coordinator*
Valerie Sprague, *Desktop Publisher*

Copyright © 1999 by the Association for Supervision and Curriculum Development. All rights reserved. No part of this publication may be reproduced or transmitted in any form or by any means, electronic or mechanical, including photocopy, recording, or any information storage and retrieval system, without permission from ASCD. Readers who wish to duplicate material copyrighted by ASCD may do so for a small fee by contacting the Copyright Clearance Center, 222 Rosewood Dr., Danvers, MA 01923, USA (telephone: 978-750-8044; fax: 978-750-4470). ASCD has authorized the CCC to collect such fees on its behalf. Requests to reprint rather than photocopy should be directed to ASCD's permissions office at 703-578-9600.

ASCD publications present a variety of viewpoints. The views expressed or implied in this book should not be interpreted as official positions of the Association.

Printed in the United States of America.

April 1999 member book (pcr). ASCD Premium, Comprehensive, and Regular members periodically receive ASCD books as part of their membership benefits. No. FY 99-6.

ASCD Stock No. 199040
ASCD member price: $17.95   nonmember price: $21.95

Library of Congress Cataloging-in-Publication Data
Tomlinson, Carol A.
   The differentiated classroom : responding to the needs of all
learners / Carol Ann Tomlinson.
     p. cm.
   Includes bibliographical references and index.
   ISBN 0-87120-342-1
   1. Individualized instruction. 2. Cognitive styles in children.
3. Mixed ability grouping in education. I. Title.
   LB1031 .T65 1999
   371.39'4—dc21
                                    99-6162
                                    CIP

06 05 04 03 02   10 9 8 7 6

The Differentiated Classroom: Responding to the Needs of All Learners

1813

104753

104753

Foreword

She waited until they were all in their usual places,
and then she asked, "Did I choose you, or did you choose
me?" And the Souls answered, "Yes!"
E. L. Konigsburg
The View from Saturday

I enjoyed writing this book because it reminded me that teaching is, in part, a history. I enjoyed writing this book because it reminded me of *my* history as a teacher.

Writing this book connected me with teachers of another century in one-room schoolhouses on the Great Plains of the United States. These teachers accepted all comers and said by their actions, "I'm grateful for every one of you who came to learn. Different as you are, we can make this work!"

This book also transported me back to late nights at the home of my first real teaching partner nearly three decades ago. She and I tried to make sense of multitask classrooms, which seemed the obvious need of our very diverse students. After three decades of a remarkable friendship, Doris Standridge still works with me to make sense of teaching—and of life. In this book, she also created all the graphics.

Writing this book led me to recall the names and faces of students I taught and who unfailingly taught me. They were high schoolers, preschoolers, and middle schoolers. They were so alike, yet so different. They needed me to be many things to them, not just one person, and they taught me how to achieve that.

This book reminded me of colleagues in Fauquier County, Va. They worked hard, took professional risks, thought "outside the box," found joy in classrooms, and created joy there, too. It was a classy school district, and it was a great training ground for teaching because there was encouragement to be an innovator.

Writing this book helped me retrace my steps on the journey of my "second life" at the University of Virginia and in schools around the country. I now work with teachers in all the different kinds of places that make up the United States and with all the sorts of students who are its future. At the University of Virginia, my colleagues push my thinking and model excellence. My students often ask, "Why?" Then generally they follow with, "Why not?" Students still are my teachers.

Around the country, other teachers' questions create thick, patterned tapestries of understanding and uncertainty, which generally is the more valuable for growth. It is a risk to name any more names. People in so many places have contributed to what I know to write here. In a few places, however, I have lingered longer, and in those places, conversations have been especially powerful.

I am grateful to Mindy Passe, Lynn Howard, the Project START teachers, and many others in the Charlotte-Mecklenburg (N.C.) Schools; to Susan Allan and the Grosse Pointe (Mich.) teachers; to Suette King and her colleagues in the Ann Arbor (Mich.) Schools; to Terry Greenlund, Sandra Page, and a large group of thoughtful teachers in the Chapel Hill-Carboro (N.C.) Schools; to Marian Gillewicz and the teachers of Yellowknife (NWT, Canada); to Pam Ungar and the principals and teachers in the Augusta County Schools (Va.); to Peg Davis and her study groups in the Madison County Schools (Va.); and to Mary Ellen Shaw, Mary Peterson, and the primary teachers at Mount Daniel Elementary School in Falls Church (Va.). I've also been enriched by interactions with principals and teachers at three research sites on differentiated instruction, where my colleagues and I have worked over the past three years: Sudbrook Middle School in the Baltimore County (Md.) Schools, Madison Middle School in the Roanoke City (Va.) Schools, and McLean Middle School in the Fort Worth (Tex.) Schools. Ideas from many folks in all these places greatly shape the pages that follow.

I have directly borrowed (I hope they don't think stolen!) lesson plans and instructional approaches from Nikki Kenney (San Antonio, Tex.); Judy Larrick (Albemarle County, Va.); Taren Basenight, Annie Joines, Jean Parrish, Nancy Brickman, and Holly Speight (Chapel Hill, N.C.); Caroline Cunningham (Peabody School, Charlottesville, Va.); Chris Stevenson (University of Vermont); and Mary Hooper and Marie deLuca (Grosse Pointe, Mich.).

I also have come to put these ideas on paper because of the partnership and support of numerous staff members at ASCD. I am particularly indebted to Leslie Kiernan, who has an unfailing heart and eye for magical classrooms and who loses sleep over any sliver of work at less than the highest quality she can produce. I also am indebted to John O'Neil, who embodies the best in teaching as an editor. He has always appreciatively accepted me where I am and asked gentle but probing questions to push me on.

Teachers often say to me, "How can I find time to differentiate instruction? I'm so busy already!" Writing this book has reinforced the only answer I know to give: "Build a career. Plan to be better tomorrow than today, but don't ever plan to be finished."

Writing this book reminded me that teaching is about learning, and that learning is about becoming, and that making a history is about making a life. This book is about writing your own history as a teacher—one day at a time, one increment of growth at a time, one collegial partnership at a time.

CAROL ANN TOMLINSON

What Is a
Differentiated Classroom?

> A different way to learn is what the kids are calling for
> . . . . All of them are talking about how our
> one-size-fits-all delivery system—which mandates that
> everyone learn the same thing at the same time, no
> matter what their individual needs—has failed them.
>
> Seymour Sarason
> *The Predictable Failure of Educational Reform*

In the United States more than a century ago, the teacher in a one-room prairie schoolhouse faced a challenging task. She had to divide her time and energy between teaching young children who had never held a book and could not read or write and teaching older, more advanced students with little interest in what the young ones were doing. Today's teachers still contend with the essential challenge of the one-room schoolhouse: how to reach out effectively to students who span the spectrum of learning readiness, personal interests, culturally shaped ways of seeing and speaking of the world, and experiences in that world.

Though today's teachers generally work with single classes with students of nearly the same age, these children have an array of needs as great as those among the children of the one-room school.

Thus, a teacher's question remains much the same as it was 100 years ago: "How do I divide time, resources, and myself so that I am an effective catalyst for maximizing talent in all my students?" Consider how these teachers answer that question.

• Mrs. Wiggins assigns students to spelling lists based on a pretest, not the assumption that all 3rd graders should work on List Three.

• Mr. Owen matches homework to student need whenever possible, trying to ensure that practice is meaningful for everyone.

• Ms. Jernigan only occasionally teaches math to the whole class at once. More often, she uses a series of direct instruction, practice, and application groups. She works hard to give everyone "equal time" at an appropriate entry point of instruction, matching practice work to student need. She also regroups students for real-world math applications so they hear a variety of voices in their journey to think mathematically.

• Ms. Enrico offers students a variety of options when it's time to create the final product for a unit. She bases the options on students' interests so they have the chance to link what they've learned with something that matters to them as individuals.

All of these teachers are differentiating instruction. Perhaps they practiced differentiating instruction before it had a name, or without even knowing its name. They are teachers who strive to do whatever it takes to ensure that struggling and advanced learners, students with varied cultural heritages, and children with different background experiences all grow as much as they possibly can each day, each week, and throughout the year.

Hallmarks of Differentiated Classrooms

In differentiated classrooms, teachers begin where students are, not the front of a curriculum guide. They accept and build upon the premise that learners differ in important ways. Thus, they also accept and act on the premise that teachers must be ready to engage students in instruction through different learning modalities, by appealing to differing interests, and by using varied rates of instruction along with varied degrees of complexity. In differentiated classrooms, teachers ensure that a student competes against himself as he grows and develops more than he competes against other students.

In differentiated classrooms, teachers provide specific ways for each individual to learn as deeply as possible and as quickly as possible, without assuming one student's road map for learning is identical to anyone else's. These teachers believe that students should be held to high standards. They work diligently to ensure that struggling, advanced, and in-between students think and work harder than they meant to; achieve more than they thought they could; and come to believe that learning involves effort, risk, and personal triumph. These teachers also work to ensure that each student consistently experiences the reality that success is likely to follow hard work.

Teachers in differentiated classes use time flexibly, call upon a range of instructional strategies, and become partners with their students to see that both what is learned and the learning environment are shaped to the learner. They do not force-fit learners into a standard mold. You might say these teachers are students of their students. They are diagnosticians, prescribing the best possible instruction for their students. These teachers also are artists who use the tools of their craft to address students' needs. They do not reach for standardized, mass-produced instruction assumed to be a good fit for all students because they recognize that students are individuals.

Teachers in differentiated classrooms begin with a clear and solid sense of what constitutes powerful curriculum and engaging instruction. Then they ask what it will take to modify that instruction so that each learner comes away with understandings and skills that offer guidance to the next phase of learning. Essentially, teachers in differentiated classrooms accept, embrace, and plan for the fact that learners bring many commonalities to school, but that learners also bring the essential differences that make them individuals. Teachers can allow for this reality in many ways to make classrooms a good fit for each individual.

Although differentiated classrooms embody common sense, they still can be difficult to achieve. In part, it is difficult to achieve a differentiated classroom because we see few examples of them. The examples that are out there, however, offer a productive way to start exploring differentiated instruction.

Portraits from Schools

Teachers work daily to find ways to reach out to individual learners at their varied points of readiness, interest, and learning preference. There is no one "right way" to create an effectively differentiated classroom; teachers craft responsive learning places in ways that are a good match for their teaching styles, as well as for learners' needs. Following are samples from classrooms in which teachers differentiate instruction. Some are lifted directly from an observation in a classroom. Some are composites of several classrooms, or extensions of conversations with teachers. All are intended to help in forming images of what it looks like and feels like in a differentiated classroom.

Snapshots from Two Primary Classrooms

For a part of each day in Mrs. Jasper's 1st grade class, students rotate among learning centers. Mrs. Jasper has worked hard for several years to provide a variety of learning centers related to several subject areas. All students go to all learning centers because Mrs. Jasper says they feel it's unfair if they don't all do the same thing. Students enjoy the movement and the independence the learning centers provide.

Many times, Isabel breezes through the center work. Just as frequently, Jamie is confused about how to do the work. Mrs. Jasper tries to help Jamie

as often as she can, but she doesn't worry so much about Isabel because her skills are well beyond those expected of a 1st grader.

Today, all students in Mrs. Jasper's class will work in a learning center on compound words. From a list of 10 compound words, they will select and illustrate 5. Later, Mrs. Jasper will ask for volunteers to show their illustrations. She will do this until the students share illustrations for all 10 words.

Down the hall, Ms. Cunningham also uses learning centers in her 1st grade classroom. She, too, has invested considerable time in developing interesting centers on a variety of subjects. Ms. Cunningham's centers, however, draw upon some of the principles of differentiated classrooms. Sometimes all students work in a particular learning center if it introduces an idea or skill new to everyone. More often, Ms. Cunningham assigns students to a specific learning center, or to a particular task at a certain learning center, based on her continually developing sense of their individual readiness.

Today, her students also will work at a learning center on compound words. Students' names are listed at the center; one of four colors is beside each name. Each student works with the folder that matches the color beside his or her name. For example, Sam has the color red next to his name. Using the materials in the red folder, Sam must decide the correct order of pairs of words to make familiar compound words. He also will make a poster that illustrates each simple word and the new compound word they form. Using materials in the blue folder, Jenna will look around the classroom and in books to find examples of compound words. She will write them out and illustrate them in a booklet. Using materials in the purple folder,

Tjuana will write a poem or a story that uses compound words she generates and that make the story or poem interesting. She then can illustrate the compound words to make the story or poem interesting to look at as well as to read. In the green folder, Dillon will find a story the teacher has written. It contains correct and incorrect compound words. Dillon will be a word detective, looking for "villains" and "good guys" among the compound words. He will create a chart to list the good guys (correct compound words) and the villains (incorrect compound words) in the story. He will illustrate the good guys and list the villains as they are in the story, and then write them correctly.

Tomorrow during circle time, all students may share what they did with their compound words. As students listen, they are encouraged to say the thing they like best about each presenter's work. Ms. Cunningham also will call on a few students who may be reticent to volunteer, asking them if they'd be willing to share what they did at the center.

Examples from Two Elementary Classrooms

In 5th grade, students at Sullins Elementary work with the concept of "famous people" to make connections between social studies and language arts. All students are expected to hone and apply research skills, to write effectively, and to share with an audience what they have learned as a result of the unit.

Mr. Elliott asks all his students to select and read a biography of a famous person from the literature or history they have studied. Students then use encyclopedias and the Internet to find out more about the person they have chosen. Each student writes a report about a famous person, describing the person's culture, childhood, education, challenges, and contributions to the world. Students are encouraged to use both original and "found" illustrations in their reports. Mr. Elliott gives a rubric to the whole class to coach students in areas such as use of research resources, organization, and quality of language.

In her 5th grade class, Mrs. May gives her students interest inventories to help them find areas where they may have a special talent or fascination, such as sports, art, medicine, the outdoors, writing, or helping others. Ultimately, each student selects an area of special interest or curiosity. The students and teacher talk about the fact that in all areas of human endeavor, famous people have shaped our understanding and practice of the field. She reads them a biographical sketch of a statesman, a musician, and an astronaut. Together, students and teacher describe principles about these famous people.

For example, famous people often are creative, they take risks to make advances in their fields, they frequently are rejected before they are admired, they sometimes fail, they sometimes succeed, and they are persistent. Students test the principles as they discuss historic figures, authors, and people in the news today. In the end, students conclude that people can be famous "for the right reasons" or "for the wrong reasons." They decide to research people who become famous by having a positive impact on the world.

The school media specialist helps each student to generate lists of "positive" famous people in that student's particular categories of interest. She also helps them learn how to locate a variety of resources that can help them research famous individuals. This includes brainstorming possible interview sources. She talks with them about the importance of selecting research materials they can read and understand clearly. She also offers to help them look for alternatives if they find materials that seem too easy or too hard for them.

Mrs. May and her students talk about how to take notes and try various ways to take notes during their research. They also consider different methods of organizing their information, such as webs, outlines, storyboards, and matrices. They talk about all the ways they can express their understandings: through essays, historical fiction, monologues, poems, caricatures, or character sketches. Mrs. May provides students with a rubric that guides them on the content, research, planning, and outcome of their work. Students also work with Mrs. May individually to set their own goals for understandings, working processes, and final products.

As the assignment continues, Mrs. May works with individuals and small groups to assess their understanding and progress and to coach them for quality. Students also assess each other's work according to the rubrics and individual goals. They ensure that each report shows someone who has made a "positive" contribution to the world. In the end, the whole class completes a mural in the cafeteria that lists the principles of fame in the shape of puzzle pieces. On each puzzle piece, students write or illustrate examples of the principle from their famous person's life. They then add ways in which they believe the principles are or will be important in their own lives. Students also share their final products with an adult who knows something about, or is interested in learning about, the person they researched.

Comparisons from the Middle Grades

In Mr. Cornell's science class, students work in a specific cycle: read the text chapter, answer questions at the end of the chapter, discuss what they have read, complete a lab, and take a quiz. Students do the labs and complete their reports in groups of four. Sometimes Mr. Cornell assigns students to a lab group as a way of managing behavior problems. Often, students select their own lab groups. They read the text and answer the questions individually. Mr. Cornell typically conducts two or three whole-class discussions during a chapter. All students enter the science fair in the spring, with a project based on a topic studied in the fall or winter.

Mrs. Santos often assigns students in her science class to reading squads when they work with text materials. At this stage, group assignments usually are made so students of similar reading levels work together. She varies graphic organizers and learning log prompts according to the amount of structure and concreteness the various groups need to grasp essential understandings from the chapter. She also makes it possible for students to read aloud in their groups or to read silently. Then they complete organizers and prompts together. As students read, Mrs. Santos moves among groups. Sometimes she reads key passages to them, sometimes she asks them to read to her, but she always probes for deeper understanding and helps to clarify their thinking.

Sometimes Mrs. Santos asks students to complete labs, watch videos, or work with supplementary materials before they read the chapter so they have a clear sense of guiding principles before they work with the text. Sometimes they read the text for awhile, do a lab, and go back to the text. Sometimes labs and supplementary materials follow text exploration. Frequently, she will have two versions of a lab going simultaneously: one for students who need concrete experiences to understand essential principles and one for students who already grasp the important principles and can deal with them in complex and uncertain contexts.

Mrs. Santos gives quizzes and diagnostic learning log entries several times in the course of a unit. Thus, she is aware of which students need additional instruction with key understandings and skills and which students need more advanced applications early in the unit. Students have several choices for a major science project:

• Work alone or with peers to investigate and address a problem in the community that relates to the science they are studying.

• Work in a mentorship role with a person or group in the community using science to address a local problem.

• Study scientists past and present who have positively influenced the practice of science in an area they have studied.

• Write a science fiction story based on the science they have studied with the goal of submitting the story to the school's literary arts anthology.

• Use classroom cameras to create a narrated photo essay that would help a younger student understand how some facet of the science they have studied works in the world.

• Propose another option to the teacher and work with her to shape a project that demonstrates understanding and skill in science.

In Mr. O'Reilly's 8th grade English class, students read the same novels and have whole-class discussions on them. Students complete journal entries on their readings.

In Mrs. Wilkerson's 8th grade English class, students often read novels around a common theme, such as courage or conflict resolution. Students select from a group of four or five novels on the

same concept, and Mrs. Wilkerson provides classroom sets of the books. Mrs. Wilkerson also makes sure the novels span a considerable reading range and tap into several interests.

Mrs. Wilkerson's 8th graders meet frequently in literature circles with students reading the same novel. There they discuss what they are reading. Although the various literature circles reflect different degrees of reading proficiency, students in each group take turns serving in one of five leadership roles: discussion director, graphic illustrator, historical investigator, literary luminary, and vocabulary enricher. There are printed guides for each role to help students fulfill them well. Mrs. Wilkerson also varies journal prompts, sometimes assigning different prompts to different students. Often, she encourages students to select a prompt that interests them. There also are many opportunities for whole-class discussion on the theme that all the novels share, allowing all students to contribute to an understanding of how the theme "plays out" in the book they are reading and in life.

Samples from High School

In Spanish I, Mrs. Horton's students complete the same language pattern drills, work on the same oral exercises, read the same passages, and take the same quizzes.

In French I, Mr. Adams's students often work with written drills at differing levels of complexity and with different amounts of teacher support. Their oral exercises focus on the same basic structures, but completion requires different levels of sophistication with the language. Sometimes students can "opt out" of review sessions to create their own French dialogue or to read a French language magazine. Students often work in teacher-assigned, mixed-readiness pairs to prepare for what the teacher calls "fundamentals quizzes." Students who wish to do so can, from time to time, select a partner to prepare for a "challenge quiz." Success on a challenge quiz nets students "homework passes" they can use to be excused from homework assignments when their work on the quiz indicates they have mastered the homework material.

In Mr. Matheson's Algebra II class, students typically complete the same homework, work independently on in-class drills, and take the same tests.

In her Algebra II class, Mrs. Wang helps students identify key concepts and skills in a given chapter. After various chapter assessments, students are encouraged to look at their own assessment results and select homework assignments and in-class miniworkshops that will help them clarify areas of confusion. She encourages students to decide whether they work most effectively alone or with a partner and to make that choice when there are opportunities to do so. Toward the end of a chapter, Mrs. Wang also gives students individual "challenge problems," which they can tackle alone or with a classmate. She designs the problems to be a mental reach. On end-of-chapter tests, students find challenge problems similar but not identical to the ones Mrs. Wang gave them earlier. There may be five or six different challenge problems distributed among the tests of 30 students.

In physical education, Mrs. Bowen's students usually all work with the same exercises and basketball drills. Mr. Wharton helps his students diagnose their starting points with various exercises and basketball skills, set challenging goals for personal improvement, and chart their personal progress. He particularly stresses growth in two areas: a student's best and weakest area.

In U.S. History, Miss Roberson and her students cover the information in the text sequentially. She lectures to supplement information in the text. Miss Roberson includes a special emphasis on women's history and African American history during the months designated by the school for those emphases.

Mrs. Washington's U.S. History students look for key concepts and generalizations that recur in each period of history they study. They also look for concepts and generalizations unique to each period. They study various points of view and the experiences shared by various cultural, economic, and gender groups. They use a variety of text, video, and taped materials of varying degrees of difficulty. Mrs. Washington sometimes lectures, but she always uses overhead transparencies that provide key points of her lecture to help visual learners. She also stops throughout the lecture to encourage students to talk about key ideas in the lecture and to ensure their grasp of those ideas. Essays and projects often ask students to take their understanding of a period in U.S. history and contrast it with what was going on in another culture and in another geographical area during the same period. Project assignments always offer several options for how a student can express his or her understanding. At the end of each quarter, students have the option of taking their whole grade from an exam, or they can take half of it from an alternative assessment proposed by the teacher and modified by the student with teacher guidance and approval.

• • •

Differentiated classrooms feel right to students who learn in different ways and at different rates and who bring to school different talents and interests. More significantly, such classrooms work better for a full range of students than do one-size-fits-all settings. Teachers in differentiated classrooms are more in touch with their students and approach teaching more as an art than as a mechanical exercise.

Developing classrooms that actively attend to both student similarities and student differences is anything but simple. The chapters that follow describe classrooms with differentiated, or responsive, instruction, and they offer guidance on how you can, over time, make such classrooms a reality for your class or school.

Elements of Differentiation

2

> The biggest mistake of past centuries in teaching has
> been to treat all children as if they were variants of the
> same individual, and thus to feel justified in teaching
> them the same subjects in the same ways.
> Howard Gardner (in Siegel & Shaughnessy, 1994)
> *Phi Delta Kappan*

Most effective teachers modify some of their instruction for students some of the time. Many of those teachers also believe they differentiate instruction, and, to some degree, they do. It is not this book's goal, however, to recount the sorts of modifications sensitive teachers make from time to time, such as offering a student extra help during lunch or asking an especially able learner a challenging question during a review session. This book offers guidance for educators who want to develop and facilitate consistent, robust plans in anticipation of and in response to students' learning differences.

Principles That Guide Differentiated Classrooms

There is no single formula for creating a differentiated classroom. What follows are a few of the key ideas about differentiation. As you read and consider them, you might want to think about your own classroom, or refer to Chapter 1 and the illustrations of differentiated classrooms to see how the principles look in action.

The Teacher Focuses on the Essentials

No one can learn everything in every textbook, let alone in a single subject. The brain is structured so that even the most able of us will forget more than we remember about most topics. It is crucial, then, for teachers to articulate what's essential for learners to recall, understand, and be able to do in a given domain.

In a differentiated classroom, the teacher carefully fashions instruction around the essential concepts, principles, and skills of each subject. She intends that students will leave the class with a firm grasp of those principles and skills, but they *won't* leave with a sense that they have conquered all there is to know. The teacher's clarity ensures that struggling learners focus on essential understandings and skills; they don't drown in a pool of disjointed facts. Similarly, the teacher ensures that advanced learners spend their time grappling with important complexities rather than repeating work on what they already know. Clarity increases the likelihood that a teacher can introduce a subject in a way that each student finds meaningful and interesting. Clarity also ensures that teacher, learners, assessment, curriculum, and instruction are linked tightly in a journey likely to culminate in personal growth and individual success for each child.

The Teacher Attends to Student Differences

From a very young age, children understand that some of us are good with kicking a ball, some with telling funny stories, some with manipulating numbers, and some with making people feel happy. They understand that some of us struggle with reading words from a page, others with keeping tempers in check, still others with arms or legs that are weak. Children seem to accept a world in which we are not alike. They do not quest for sameness, but they search for the sense of triumph that comes when they are respected, valued, nurtured, and even cajoled into accomplishing things they believed beyond their grasp.

In differentiated classrooms, the teacher is well aware that human beings share the same basic needs for nourishment, shelter, safety, belonging, achievement, contribution, and fulfillment. She also knows that human beings find those things in different fields of endeavor, according to different timetables, and through different paths. She understands that by attending to human differences she can best help individuals address their common needs. Our experiences, culture, gender, genetic codes, and neurological wiring all affect how and what we learn. In a differentiated classroom, the teacher unconditionally accepts students as they are, and she expects them to become all they can be.

Assessment and Instruction Are Inseparable

In a differentiated classroom, assessment is ongoing and diagnostic. Its goal is to provide teachers day-to-day data on students' readiness for particular ideas and skills, their interests, and their learning profiles. These teachers don't see assessment as something that comes at the end of a unit to find out what students learned; rather, assessment is today's means of understanding how to modify tomorrow's instruction.

Such formative assessment may come from small-group discussion with the teacher and a few students, whole-class discussion, journal entries, portfolio entries, exit cards, skill inventories, pretests, homework assignments, student opinion, or interest surveys. At this stage, assessment yields an emerging picture of who understands key ideas and who can perform targeted skills, at what levels of proficiency, and with what degree of interest. The teacher then shapes tomorrow's lesson—and even today's—with the goal of helping individual students move ahead from their current position of competency.

At benchmark points in learning, such as the end of a chapter or unit, teachers in differentiated classrooms use assessment to formally record student growth. Even then, however, they seek varied means of assessment so that all students can fully display their skills and understandings. Assessment always has more to do with helping students grow than with cataloging their mistakes.

The Teacher Modifies Content, Process, and Products

By thoughtfully using assessment data, the teacher can modify content, process, or product. *Content* is what she wants students to learn and the materials or mechanisms through which that is accomplished. *Process* describes activities designed to ensure that students use key skills to make sense out of essential ideas and information. *Products* are vehicles through which students demonstrate and extend what they have learned.

Students vary in readiness, interest, and learning profile. *Readiness* is a student's entry point relative to a particular understanding or skill. Students with less-developed readiness may need

• someone to help them identify and make up gaps in their learning so they can move ahead;

• more opportunities for direct instruction or practice;

• activities or products that are more structured or more concrete, with fewer steps, closer to their own experiences, and calling on simpler reading skills; or

• a more deliberate pace of learning.
Advanced students, on the other hand, may need

• to skip practice with previously mastered skills and understandings;

• activities and products that are quite complex, open-ended, abstract, and multifaceted, drawing on advanced reading materials; or

• a brisk pace of work, or perhaps a slower pace to allow for greater depth of exploration of a topic.

Interest refers to a child's affinity, curiosity, or passion for a particular topic or skill. One student may be eager to learn about fractions because she is very interested in music, and her math teacher shows her how fractions relate to music. Another child may find a study of the American Revolution fascinating because he is particularly interested in medicine and has been given the option of creating a final product on medicine during that period.

Learning profile has to do with how we learn. It may be shaped by intelligence preferences, gender, culture, or learning style. Some students need to talk ideas over with peers to learn them well. Others work better alone and with writing. Some students learn easily part-to-whole. Others need to see the big picture before specific parts make sense. Some students prefer logical or analytical approaches to learning. Other classmates prefer creative, application-oriented lessons. (See the Appendix and the end of this chapter for sources to learn more about readiness, interest, and learning profile.)

Teachers may adapt one or more of the curricular elements (content, process, products) based on one or more of the student characteristics (readiness, interest, learning profile) at any point in a lesson or unit. However, you need not differentiate all elements in all possible ways. Effective differentiated classrooms include many times in which whole-class, nondifferentiated fare is the order of the day. Modify a curricular element only when (1) you see a student need and (2) you are convinced that modification increases the likelihood that the learner will understand important ideas and use important skills more thoroughly as a result.

All Students Participate in Respectful Work

In differentiated classrooms, certain essential understandings and skills are goals for all learners. However, some students need repeated experiences to master them, and other students master them swiftly. The teacher in a differentiated classroom understands that she does not show respect for students by ignoring their learning differences. She continually tries to understand what individual students need to learn most effectively, and she attempts to provide learning options that are a good fit for each learner whenever she can. She shows respect for learners by honoring both their commonalities and differences, not by treating them alike.

For example, some students grasp an idea best when they see it directly tethered to their own lives and experiences. Others can think about the idea more conceptually. Some students strive for accuracy and eschew the uncertainty of creativity. Others thirst for the adventure of divergence and deplore the tedium of drill. Some students want to sing their understanding of a story, some want to dance the story's theme, some want to draw it, and some want to write to the author or a character.

In the end, it is not standardization that makes a classroom work. It is a deep respect for the identity of the individual. A teacher in a differentiated classroom embraces at least the following four beliefs.

- Respect the readiness level of each student.
- Expect all students to grow, and support their continual growth.
- Offer all students the opportunity to explore essential understandings and skills at degrees of difficulty that escalate consistently as they develop their understanding and skill.
- Offer all students tasks that look—and are—equally interesting, equally important, and equally engaging.

The Teacher and Students Collaborate in Learning

Teachers are the chief architects of learning, but students should assist with the design and building. It is the teacher's job to know what constitutes essential learning, to diagnose, to prescribe, to vary the instructional approach based on a variety of purposes, to ensure smooth functioning of the classroom, and to see that time is used wisely. Nonetheless, students have much to contribute about their understanding.

Students can provide diagnostic information, develop classroom rules, participate in the governing process grounded in those rules, and learn to use time as a valuable resource. Students can let teachers know when materials or tasks are too hard or too easy, when learning is interesting (and when it isn't), when they need help, and when they are ready to work alone. When they are partners in shaping all parts of the classroom experience, students develop ownership in their learning and become more skilled at understanding themselves and making choices that enhance their learning.

In a differentiated classroom, the teacher is the leader, but like all effective leaders, she attends closely to her followers and involves them thoroughly in the journey. Together, teacher and students plan, set goals, monitor progress, analyze successes and failures, and seek to multiply the successes and learn from failures. Some decisions apply to the class as a whole. Others are specific to an individual.

A differentiated classroom is, of necessity, student-centered. Students are the workers. The teacher coordinates time, space, materials, and activities. Her effectiveness increases as students become more skilled at helping one another and themselves achieve group and individual goals.

The Teacher Balances Group and Individual Norms

In many classrooms, a student is an "unsuccessful" 5th grader if he falls short of 5th grade "standards." That the student grew more than anyone in the room counts for little if he still lags behind grade-level expectations. Similarly, a child is expected to remain in 5th grade even though she achieved those standards two years ago. About that student we often say, "She's fine on her own. She's already doing well."

Teachers in a differentiated classroom understand group norms. They also understand individual norms. When a student struggles as a learner, the teacher has two goals. One is to accelerate the student's skills and understanding as rapidly as possible for that learner, still ensuring genuine understanding and meaningful application of skills. The second is to ensure that the student and parents are aware of the learner's individual goals and growth and the student's relative standing in the class. The same is true when a learner has advanced beyond grade-level expectations.

A great coach never achieves greatness for himself or his team by working to make all his players alike. To be great, and to make his players great, he must make each player the best that he or she possibly can be. No weakness in understanding or skill is overlooked. Every player plays from his or her competencies, not from a sense of deficiency. There is no such thing as "good enough" for any team member. In an effectively differentiated classroom, assessment, instruction, feedback, and grading take into account both group and individual goals and norms.

The Teacher and Students Work Together Flexibly

As in an orchestra composed of individuals, varied ensemble groups, sections, and soloists, the differentiated classroom is built around individuals, various small groups, and the class as a whole. They all work to "learn and play the score," albeit with varied instruments, solo parts, and roles in the whole.

To address the various learning needs that make up the whole, teachers and students work together in a variety of ways. They use materials flexibly and employ flexible pacing. Sometimes the entire class works together, but sometimes small groups are more effective. Sometimes everyone uses the same materials, but it is often effective to have many materials available. Sometimes everyone finishes a task at 12:15, but often some students finish a task while others need additional time for completion. Sometimes the teacher says who will work together. Sometimes students make the choice. When the teacher decides, she may do so based on similar readiness, interest, or learning profile needs. Sometimes she places students of differing readiness, interests, or learning profiles together. Sometimes assignment to tasks is random. Sometimes the teacher is the primary helper of students. Sometimes students are one another's best source of help.

In a differentiated classroom, the teacher also draws on a wide range of instructional strategies that help her focus on individuals and small groups, not just the whole class. Sometimes she finds learning contracts helpful in targeting instruction; at other times, independent investigations work well. The goal is to link learners with essential understandings and skills at appropriate levels of challenge and interest.

Two Organizers for Thinking About Differentiation

Figure 2.1 presents an organizer for thinking about differentiation, and it is a way of thinking about this book as well. In a differentiated classroom, a teacher makes consistent efforts to respond to students' learning needs. She is guided by general principles of facilitating a classroom in which attention to individuals is effective. Then she systematically modifies content, process, or product based on students' readiness for the particular topic, materials, or skills; personal interests; and learning profiles. To do so, she calls upon a range of instructional and management strategies.

The teacher does not try to differentiate everything for everyone every day. That's impossible, and it would destroy a sense of wholeness in the class. Instead, the teacher selects moments in the instructional sequence to differentiate, based on formal or informal assessment. She also selects a time in her teaching plans to differentiate by interest so that students can link what is being studied to something that is important to them. She often provides options that make it natural for some students to work alone and others together, for some to have a more hands-on approach to making sense of ideas and for others to arrive at learning in a visual way. Differentiation is an organized yet flexible way of proactively adjusting teaching and learning to meet kids where they are and help

them to achieve maximum growth as learners.

All classrooms are multifaceted. A differentiated classroom, however, differs in key ways when compared with traditional classrooms. Figure 2.2 (p. 16) suggests some ways in which the two approaches to teaching may vary. Feel free to add your own comparisons to the chart as you think about your own classroom and as you read through the rest of the book. Remember that there is much middle ground between an absolutely traditional classroom and an absolutely differentiated one (assuming either extreme could ever exist). For an interesting self-assessment, think of the two columns in the chart as continuums. Place an X on each continuum where you believe your teaching is now, and place an X on where you'd like it to be.

For More Information

To learn more about the concept of differentiating instruction through readiness, interest, and learning profile, see the Appendix and the following sources:

Kiernan, L. (producer) (1997). *Differentiating instruction: A video staff development set.* Alexandria, VA: ASCD.

Tomlinson, C. (1995). *How to differentiate instruction in mixed ability classrooms.* Alexandria, VA: ASCD.

Tomlinson, C. (1996). Good teaching for one and all: Does gifted education have an instructional identity? *Journal for the Education of the Gifted, 20,* 155-174.

Tomlinson, C. (1996). *Differentiating instruction for mixed-ability classrooms.* [An ASCD professional inquiry kit]. Alexandria, VA: ASCD.

Figure 2.1
Differentiation of Instruction

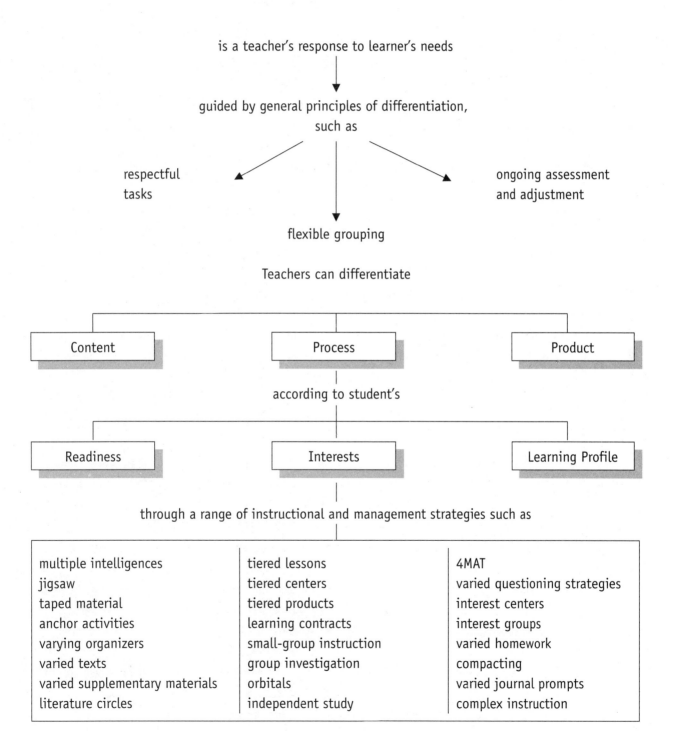

is a teacher's response to learner's needs

guided by general principles of differentiation,
such as

respectful
tasks

flexible grouping

ongoing assessment
and adjustment

Teachers can differentiate

| Content | Process | Product |

according to student's

| Readiness | Interests | Learning Profile |

through a range of instructional and management strategies such as

multiple intelligences	tiered lessons	4MAT
jigsaw	tiered centers	varied questioning strategies
taped material	tiered products	interest centers
anchor activities	learning contracts	interest groups
varying organizers	small-group instruction	varied homework
varied texts	group investigation	compacting
varied supplementary materials	orbitals	varied journal prompts
literature circles	independent study	complex instruction

Figure 2.2
Comparing Classrooms

Traditional Classroom	Differentiated Classroom
• Student differences are masked or acted upon when problematic	• Student differences are studied as a basis for planning
• Assessment is most common at the end of learning to see "who got it"	• Assessment is ongoing and diagnostic to understand how to make instruction more responsive to learner need
• A relatively narrow sense of intelligence prevails	• Focus on multiple forms of intelligences is evident
• A single definition of excellence exists	• Excellence is defined in large measure by individual growth from a starting point
• Student interest is infrequently tapped	• Students are frequently guided in making interest-based learning choices
• Relatively few learning profile options are taken into account	• Many learning profile options are provided for
• Whole-class instruction dominates	• Many instructional arrangements are used
• Coverage of texts and curriculum guides drives instruction	• Student readiness, interest, and learning profile shape instruction
• Mastery of facts and skills out-of-context are the focus of learning	• Use of essential skills to make sense of and understand key concepts and principles is the focus of learning
• Single option assignments are the norm	• Multi-option assignments are frequently used
• Time is relatively inflexible	• Time is used flexibly in accordance with student need
• A single text prevails	• Multiple materials are provided
• Single interpretations of ideas and events may be sought	• Multiple perspectives on ideas and events are routinely sought
• The teacher directs student behavior	• The teacher facilitates students' skills at becoming more self-reliant learners
• The teacher solves problems	• Students help other students and the teacher solve problems
• The teacher provides whole-class standards for grading	• Students work with the teacher to establish both whole-class and individual learning goals
• A single form of assessment is often used	• Students are assessed in multiple ways

Rethinking How We Do School—and for Whom

3

> The aim is clear. Each child—each of the
> young—should be able to advance to full capacity in
> accordance with general and special ability and aptitude.
> Paul Brandwein
> *Memorandum: On Renewing Schooling and Education*

Some may think that differentiating instruction is a recently hatched idea from wherever it is that educational "innovations" begin. Actually, it is a natural outgrowth of a burgeoning understanding of the ways children learn. A brief background on the evolution of teaching and learning over recent decades is useful for understanding what we now call "differentiating instruction."

Even Education Changes

Think back 75 or 100 years ago. Now, fast-forward to today. In many ways, those years reflect more change for humans than all the years before in recorded history. Think about farming 100 years ago—and today. Think about the practice of medicine 100 years ago—and today. Imagine

transportation 100 years ago—and today. Consider the 20th century's changes in engineering, clothing, and communication. The transformation is dizzying! While most of us succumb to occasional nostalgia for "the good old days," few of us would opt for yesterday's physicians, communication systems, or fashion.

Although we think of school as a static enterprise, the field of education has grown and changed, too. Today we understand many things about teaching and learning that we had no way of knowing a century, or even a few decades, ago. Some of these insights stem from psychology and the science of the brain. Others come from continuing observation in classrooms. Whatever their genesis, these educational changes are every bit as revolutionary as moving from the pencil to the typewriter to the personal computer.

17

New Ways of Thinking About School

We could fill volumes with the expanding understandings of how children learn. We could fill other volumes with the implications of this knowledge for teachers. That is not the goal of this book, but it is important to sketch out a few recent, pivotal insights about teaching and learning.

Differentiated instruction is first and foremost good instruction. Many current understandings about learning provide strong support for classrooms that recognize, honor, and cultivate individuality. Following are three principles of effective teaching and learning that educators have not always known or clearly supported.

Intelligence Is Variable

We can draw at least three important conclusions from the study of intelligence over the past half century. First, intelligence is multifaceted, not a single thing. Howard Gardner (1991, 1993, 1997) suggests that humans have eight intelligences: verbal-linguistic, logical-mathematical, visual-spatial, bodily-kinesthetic, musical-rhythmic, interpersonal, intrapersonal, and naturalistic. Robert Sternberg (1985, 1988, 1997) suggests three kinds of intelligences: analytical, practical, and creative. Before them, other researchers, such as Thorndike, Thurstone, and Guilford (Horowitz & O'Brien, 1985), identified varied types of intelligence. While the names of intelligences vary, educators, psychologists, and researchers have drawn two significant, consistent conclusions:

- We think, learn, and create in different ways.
- Development of our potential is affected by the match between what we learn and how we learn with our particular intelligences.

A second important conclusion about intelligence is that it is fluid, not fixed. In other words, providing children with rich learning experiences can amplify their intelligence, and denying them such richness of experience can diminish their intelligence (Caine & Caine, 1991).

A third understanding stems from the burgeoning field of brain research (Caine & Caine, 1991; Sylwester, 1995). Neurons grow and develop when they are used actively; they atrophy when they are not used. Vigorous learning changes the physiology of the brain.

These theories suggest several clear implications for educators. For example, teachers must be effective in developing many types of intelligence, not just one. Also, students who come to school lacking rich learning experiences can make up lost ground if they find rich experiences in their classrooms. All students must continue vigorous, new learning, or they risk losing brain power.

The Brain Hungers for Meaning

Thanks to progress with imaging technology in the field of medicine, we can now look inside the human brain and see how it functions. Such observations have rapidly expanded the understanding of teaching and learning. We now know important details about what works best for the brain in learning (Caine & Caine, 1991, 1994, 1997; Jensen, 1998; Kalbfleisch, 1997; Sylwester, 1995).

The brain seeks meaningful patterns and resists meaninglessness. Though the brain retains isolated or disparate bits of information, it is much more efficient at retaining information that is "chunked." Chunked information is organized around categories and ideas that increase the information's meaningfulness. The brain constantly seeks to connect parts to wholes, and individuals learn by connecting something new to something they already understand.

The brain learns best when it can come to understand by making its own sense out of information rather than when information is imposed on it. The brain doesn't respond much to things that carry only a surface meaning. It responds far more effectively and efficiently to something that carries deep and personal meaning, something that is life shaping, relevant, important, or taps into emotions.

These and many other understandings tell us much about the individuality of learners and about the nature of effective curriculum and instruction. Brain research tells us that each learner's brain is unique, and educators must provide many opportunities for varied learners to make sense of ideas and information. The research tells us that when we set out to have students connect the novel to the familiar, what is novel to one child already may be familiar to another and vice versa.

Brain research tells us that curriculum must cultivate meaning making. It should be organized around categories, concepts, and governing principles. A meaningful curriculum is characterized by high interest and high relevance, and it taps into learners' feelings and experiences. If we want students to retain, understand, and use ideas, information, and skills, we must give them ample opportunity to make sense of, or "own," them through involvement in complex learning situations.

Brain research also makes clear that if learning is a process of connecting the unfamiliar to the familiar, teachers must create abundant opportunities for students to link the new with the old. This is a three-part task. First, teachers must identify the essential concepts, principles, and skills of their subjects. Then they must become experts about their students' learning needs. Then they must use this information about learning needs to provide differentiated opportunities for students to construct understanding by connecting what they know with the essentials they are trying to learn.

Humans Learn Best with Moderate Challenge

Through increased understanding of both psychology and the brain, we now know that individuals learn best when they are in a context that provides a moderate challenge (Bess, 1997; Csikszentmihalyi, Rathunde, & Whalen, 1993; Howard, 1994; Jensen, 1998; Vygotsky, 1978, 1986). That is, when a task is far too difficult for a learner, the learner feels threatened and "downshifts" into a self-protection mode. A threatened learner will not persist with thinking or problem solving. On the other hand, a simple task also suppresses a learner's thinking and problem solving. He or she coasts into a relaxation mode.

A task is appropriately challenging when it asks learners to risk a leap into the unknown, but they know enough to get started and have additional support for reaching a new level of understanding. Put another way, students who consistently fail lose their motivation to learn. Students who succeed too easily also lose their motivation to learn. For learning to continue, students must believe that hard work is required, but the hard work often pays off with success. Teachers also must remember that what is moderately challenging today won't offer the same challenge tomorrow. Challenges must grow as students grow in their learning.

Again, this new knowledge offers important guidance for educators. What is moderately challenging and motivating for one learner may offer far too little challenge (and therefore little motivation) for a classmate. The same task just may be too stressful for yet another classmate. Learning tasks must be adjusted to each student's appropriate learning zone. Further, tasks must escalate in complexity and challenge for students to learn continually.

Thinking About the Students We Teach

Over the past half century or more, the student population has changed dramatically. Today, all children are expected to come to school, whatever their gender, socioeconomic status, or physical or mental challenge. Yet at one time, not all children came to public school. Children with physical disabilities and severe learning problems stayed home. Children from poor homes, including new immigrants, worked in factories or at other jobs to help support the family. Farm children worked the fields and didn't come to school, except in seasons when crops didn't require planting or harvesting. Girls were often excluded from advanced education because of the perception that they would marry, raise children, and run a household, roles not believed to require much education. Children of the very rich often had tutors or went to exclusive boarding schools.

Not too long ago, most children who came to school had two parents in the home. At least one of those parents usually was at home when the child left for school and when the child returned. We now teach many children whose homes have only one parent. Most children no longer have a parent at home at both ends of the school day. While that fact alone is not necessarily negative, it complicates children's lives. Sometimes children are frightened by this isolation. Many lack a steady hand to monitor school progress or homework—or even to listen to the events of a school day.

We teach children who, for better or worse (and probably both), are offspring of the electronic era. Their world is both larger and smaller. They know more things, but they understand less of what they know. They are accustomed to quick and ready entertainment, and yet their imaginations are less active. They have to cope with realities and problems that once would have been unknown to children, and yet many have markedly smaller support systems for wisely navigating these problems. They are aware of all sorts of positive possibilities in the adult world, but they have little sense of how to build bridges to reach them. These young people are at ease with and itchy to use technologies that frighten many of the adults "in charge" of their worlds.

Today, more kinds of children come to school and stay in school, bringing with them a greater range of backgrounds and needs. Many of these children lack the "givens" of early life that a teacher once took for granted. They are at once enriched and impoverished by their environments. Further, there is a chasm between children who have benefited from rich childhood experiences and those who haven't had the same opportunities.

The Struggle for Equity and Excellence

Many of today's students come from homes where support and encouragement are in short supply. These children have immense learning potential, but they arrive at school with that potential weighted down by a lack of experience, support, models, and plans that, if present, would make education a fundamental expectation of life.

On the other hand, many other learners come to school with skills and knowledge months or years ahead of where their learning is "expected" to be according to the standard curriculum.

Schools must belong to all of these children. Educators often speak of equity as an issue with children of the former group and excellence as an issue for the latter. In truth, equity and excellence must be at the top of the agenda for all children.

We cannot achieve equity for children who come to school at risk of falling behind in learning unless we ensure that these learners enter classrooms where teachers are ready to help build the sorts of experiences and expectations that the world outside the classroom may have been unable to build for the child. We cannot achieve excellence for children at risk of school failure without emphatically, systematically, vigorously, and effectively seeing to the development of their full potential. We must dream big dreams with them and be persistent partners in helping them soar toward those dreams. Both equity and excellence must be a part of our road map for these students.

Similarly, children who come to school advanced beyond grade expectations in one or more areas also require equity of opportunity to grow from their points of entry, with teachers doggedly determined to ensure that their potential does not languish. These children, too, need teachers who commend, and command, excellence—teachers who help them dream big, who cause them to experience, accept, and embrace personal challenge. Both equity and excellence must be a part of our road map for these students as well.

Every child is entitled to the promise of a teacher's enthusiasm, time, and energy. All children are entitled to teachers who will do everything in their power to help them realize their potential every day. It is unacceptable for any teacher to respond to any group of children (or any individual child) as though the children were inappropriate, inconvenient, beyond hope, or not in need of focused attention.

Grouping and the Quest for Equity and Excellence

Schools have tried to meet the needs of struggling and advanced learners by pulling them from regular classrooms for part or all of the school day. They were assigned to special classrooms with similar students and teachers who have the knowledge and skill to meet their unique needs. In full accord with common sense and classroom experience, much of the best research suggests that for struggling learners, such homogeneous learning experiences go awry (e.g., Oakes, 1985; Slavin, 1987, 1993). Too often in these settings, teachers' expectations for the struggling learners decline, materials are simplified, the level of discourse is less than sterling, and the pace slackens. Too few students escape these arrangements to join more "typical," or advanced, classes. In other words, remedial classes keep remedial learners remedial.

Also in full accord with common sense and classroom experience, much of the best research (Allan, 1991; Kulik & Kulik, 1991) suggests that when we place advanced learners in accelerated, homogeneous classes, they benefit from a brisk pace, stimulating discourse, raised teacher expectations, and enriched materials. In other words, they continue to advance.

In theory, creating heterogeneous classes should address equity and excellence for all learners. There are three major flaws in that assumption, at least as schools have practiced it to this point.

First, struggling learners will not experience more long-term success by being placed in heterogeneous classes unless we are ready and able to meet them at their points of readiness and systematically escalate their learning until they are able to function as competently and confidently as other learners. We have often claimed that such heterogeneous classes represent high expectations for struggling learners, but we then leave them to their own devices to figure out how to "catch up" with the expectations. Such an approach does not result in genuine growth for struggling learners.

Advanced learners highlight a second, similar, problem. Once in a heterogeneous classroom, advanced students often are asked to do a greater volume of work that they already know how to do, to ensure the success of other students through much of the school day by serving as peer coaches, or to wait (patiently, of course) while students with less advanced skills continue to work for mastery of skills already mastered by the advanced learner. Implicitly, and sometimes even explicitly, we suggest that advanced learners are fine without special provisions because they are "up to standards" already. Again, this approach won't achieve genuine growth for advanced learners.

A third problem with heterogeneity, as it is typically practiced, is the assumption that what happens in heterogeneous classrooms for "typical learners" is what it needs to be. Our premise has been that everyone can benefit from standard classrooms. In fact, it is often the case that what is standard is far less than the best we know to do, even for "standard" students.

When we create effective communities of learning in which the needs of all learners are specifically and systematically addressed, we will go a long way toward addressing both equity and excellence in schools. However, heterogeneity usually is a one-size-fits-all endeavor where the learning plan swallows some learners and pinches others. Such classes provide for neither equity nor excellence.

Old Ways of Doing School—Still Alive and Afoot

Despite compelling new educational knowledge, classrooms have changed little over the last 100 years. We still assume that a child of a given age is enough like all other children of the same age that he or she should traverse the same curriculum in the same fashion with all other students of that age. Further, schools act as though all children should finish classroom tasks as near to the same moment as possible. A school year should be the same length for all learners. To this end, schools generally adopt a single textbook, give students a single test at the end of the chapter, and another test at the end of designated marking periods. Teachers use the same grading system for all children of a given age and grade, whatever their starting point at the beginning of the year.

The curriculum typically is based on goals that involve having students accumulate and retain a variety of facts and skills that are far removed from any meaningful context. Drill-and-practice worksheets are the chief educational technology, and teachers tell students things they must then tell back, a legacy of behaviorism rooted firmly in the 1930s. Teachers still largely "run" classes, and they are likely to work harder and more actively than students much of the time.

To the degree that we focus on developing intelligence in schools, educators seem convinced that only narrow, analytical slices of verbal and computational intelligence are important. This is almost the same as nearly a century ago when the public believed that a bit of reading, writing, and computation would serve learners well in an adulthood dominated by assembly line and agrarian jobs. Schools still prepare children for tests more than for life. Sometimes, cartoonists make the point more powerfully than serious prose, as shown in Figure 3.1.

Many observers have written wisely and well about why schools seem so resistant to change (e.g., Caine & Caine, 1997; Eisner, 1994; Fullan & Stiegelbauer, 1991; Fullan, 1993; Sarason, 1990, 1993). The point here is that while the rest of the world seized upon progress over the last century, the *practice* of education remained static. To overcome this, we need to begin our investigation of how to differentiate instruction for a diverse

Figure 3.1

Calvin and Hobbes © 1993 Watterson. Reprinted with permission of Universal Press Syndicate. All rights reserved.

student population with some important assumptions.

• Students differ in experience, readiness, interest, intelligences, language, culture, gender, and mode of learning. As one elementary teacher noted, "Children already come to us differentiated. It just makes sense that we would differentiate our instruction in response to them."

• To maximize the potential in each learner, educators need to meet each child at his or her starting point and ensure substantial growth during each school term.

• Classrooms that ignore student differences are unlikely to maximize potential in any student who differs significantly from the "norm." This is an issue even in "homogeneous" classrooms where student variance is inevitably great.

• To ensure maximum student growth, teachers need to make modifications for students rather than assume students must modify themselves to fit the curriculum. In fact, children do not know how to differentiate their own curriculum successfully.

• Best-practice education should be the starting point for differentiation. It makes little sense to modify practices that defy the best understanding of teaching and learning. As noted educator Seymour Sarason (1990) reminds us, any classroom efforts that aren't powered by an understanding of what keeps children eagerly pursuing knowledge are doomed to fail.

• Classrooms grounded in best-practice education, and modified to be responsive to student differences, benefit virtually all students. Differentiation addresses the needs of struggling and advanced learners. It addresses the needs of students for whom English is a second language and students who have strong learning style preferences. It addresses gender differences and cultural differences. It pays homage to the truth that we are not born to become replicas of one another.

As Howard Gardner (1997) suggests, even if we could figure out how to make everyone a brilliant violinist, an orchestra also needs top-quality musicians who play woodwinds, brass, percussion, and strings. Differentiation is about high-quality performance for all individuals and giving students the opportunity to develop their particular strengths.

Learning Environments That Support Differentiated Instruction

4

A really good teacher is someone who: knows that a
student can teach and a teacher can learn, integrates
him[self] or herself into the learning environment,
literally taking a seat among the conglomerate of desks,
proving that he or she enjoys associating with the minds
made of sponges, ready to absorb, appreciates that what
one thinks and says is more important than what one
uses to fill in the blanks.

Krista, Age 17
Jane Bluestein, Editor
Mentors, Masters and Mrs. MacGregor:
Stories of Teachers Making a Difference

Not long ago, a teacher asked me an intriguing question. Her inquiry was earnest—and I responded accordingly—but I have refashioned my answer to her dozens of times since I left the place we shared for a day. Her question was, "Is it possible to differentiate instruction in a class where all the students sit in rows and where most of their work is done alone and in silence?"

Her brow was furrowed when she asked the question, and I'm sure mine was furrowed as I replied, "Yes, I think you could apply many principles of differentiated instruction in that setting. You could still offer students appropriately challenging content. You could offer activities at levels that provide moderate challenge for different students. You could offer product assignments that wrap around individual interests and intelligence strengths."

I paused and added, "You'd have difficulty with students whose learning styles are itchy for collaboration, conversation, and movement."

Another pause. "But if I had a choice between a class in which everyone sat silently in straight rows and worked on the same things, in the same way, over the same time spans—or one in which they all sat silently in straight rows and worked on tasks at appropriate degrees of difficulty and with links to their interests—I'd opt for the latter in a heartbeat."

I did go on to say that having only those two options limited both teacher and students. I did not stop in my tracks and say, "Much of what we're talking about here loses its power if the classroom environment is defective."

The teacher who asked the question was "asking between the lines." That is, her words posed only part of her question. She really was saying something like, "Okay: I know I have students who come to me at varying points of readiness for my curriculum. I know I'm losing many of them from confusion or boredom. I can even accept that tapping into student interests and learning profiles could help them learn more effectively. I can go along with you on much of that. I don't think I can give up my image of the lady in front of the room who runs a tight ship. You're already suggesting that the way I look at my curriculum should change. Surely you're not asking me to reconstruct my image of myself as a teacher, too!"

I haven't changed my mind about what I said to this teacher. I still think that student tasks should focus on essential understandings and skills. The tasks should be presented in varying ways so that each student has to stretch beyond his or her comfort zone. These kinds of tasks are far preferable to "standard issue" work. It's just that I also believe so much more about the pervasive importance of classroom environment than I was alert enough to say that day. This teacher was asking me if it

makes sense to cure a patient's cold when the patient also has a badly broken leg. Yes, it does. But without a healed leg, the patient still suffers from pain, distress, and a hobbled life.

The rest of this chapter contains some of what I could have said to this teacher. It is pivotal to the concept of differentiated instruction. Children, teachers, and classrooms come together as microcosms of human existence. In unhealthy microcosms, some good things still happen. Great things, however, consistently come from robust, healthy places.

Teaching as a Learning Triangle

I once watched a young, bright, dedicated math teacher engage in an unspoken battle with his disenchanted students. The teacher's knowledge of geometry was deep and broad. His activities were relevant and intriguing. Yet his adolescent students vacillated between detachment and hostility. What should have been an exemplary class was rife with unspoken animosity. I watched the situation for what seemed eternity, and I was as happy as the teacher and students when the bell delivered us all from more suffering.

"Why isn't it working?" he asked me later. "What's wrong?"

Like many teachers, I never had many occasions to state explicitly my beliefs about creating a learning environment. I just taught day after day, trying to build on what worked and eliminate what didn't. I think my answer to this teacher, however, was an important verbalization of what my students and colleagues had taught me during two decades in the classroom.

"Artful teaching is a like a learning triangle," I responded. "It's an equilateral triangle with the teacher, the kids, and the 'stuff' at each point. If any side goes unattended and gets out of balance with the others, the artfulness is lost."

This young geometry teacher had problems with two of the legs of the triangle (see Figure 4.1). While he knew the content brilliantly, he was insecure and didn't have a deep devotion to his kids. As a result, he was a peacock in his classroom, strutting about with a show designed to convince his students (and himself) that he was a hot commodity. A one-sided triangle—a triangle with only the content—isn't a triangle at all.

It's important to understand what probably should happen with, for, and among students, teachers, and the content in a classroom. Then teacher and students together can construct the sort of environment that strengthens the learning triangle.

The Top of the Triangle

By its definition, an equilateral triangle is a geometric figure with three equal sides. Thus, technically, it has no top, since any one point of the

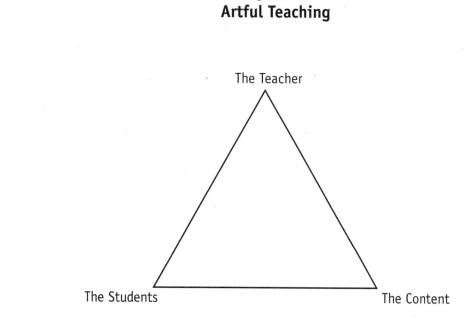

Figure 4.1
Artful Teaching

The Teacher

The Students

The Content

Consider teaching and learning as a triangle, in which all parts are needed to create and support the whole.

triangle can be the "top." For our purposes, however, the teacher has to be atop the learning triangle.

The teacher is the inevitable leader in any effective classroom. Leadership can and should be shared with the learners, but responsibility for the leadership resides with the adult who is charged by professionalism, tradition, and law with that task. A teacher who plays that leadership role effectively must be secure about himself—must like himself. A teacher who is essentially insecure about himself is unlikely to create a climate of acceptance an affirmation between himself and the students, or among the students. That does not mean a secure teacher lacks doubts, is free of uncertainty, or is unwavering in direction. Quite the contrary: The variables in a classroom are so great they make uncertainty both inevitable and proper.

Instead, a secure teacher expects to be a learner all day, every day, and he is comfortable with the ambiguity of that role. It's not so important to be right as to be open. It's not so important to have all the answers as to be hungry for them. A secure teacher comes away from today with important questions to puzzle about overnight and the belief that today contains the insights necessary for a more effective tomorrow. A secure teacher believes that having these kinds of insights is professionally challenging and personally satisfying.

Further, the secure teacher accepts the reality that he controls the climate in the classroom. His approach to students and instruction determines whether respect, humiliation, delight, drudgery, possibility, or defeat wins the day. He knows that he will err some days, but he also knows that he has the capacity and responsibility to avoid the same error another day.

Bob Strachota (1996) reflects what it means to be a teacher who knows he does not have all the answers—but that he has the power to find them.

> Neither my life in school nor my life away from school is particularly blissful. My car breaks down, I quarrel with my friends, I get sick, and I worry about my children. I have to keep a watch on my moods, needs, biases, weaknesses, and limits in order to see how they are affecting my work. If I can monitor how my emotions are at play in my classroom, I can better put a brake on them when they are destructive, and better allow my joyful, level, nurturant side to dominate (p. 75).

Strachota's primary goal is to develop students' capacity to take control of their own lives and learning. He also is aware that he is atop the learning triangle in facilitating that end.

Students in a Healthy Classroom

Mary Ann Smith is one of my mentors. She doesn't know that, because she moved away before I had the sense to tell her. She taught primary students when I taught early adolescents, but the students' age difference is irrelevant. What she knows is essential whether the learner is 5 or 55.

Every year, Mary Ann's principal gave her a hefty supply of misfits. I often received those students five or six years later. As I listened to their parents talk, I realized that the only year those youngsters felt comfortable in school was the year they had Mrs. Smith.

The mother of four boys, Mary Ann simply created a classroom in much the same way she created her home. Here are some things she knew about kids in both places.

• Each kid is like all others and different from all others.

• Kids need unconditional acceptance as human beings.

• Kids need to believe they can become something better than they are.

• Kids need help in living up to their dreams.

• Kids have to make their own sense of things.

• Kids often make their own sense of things more effectively and coherently when adults collaborate with them.

• Kids need action, joy, and peace.

• Kids need power over their lives and learning.

• Kids need help to develop that power and use it wisely.

• Kids need to be secure in a larger world.

Mary Ann's goal with her own sons was to make each of them whole, happy, and independent. She adored each boy, as much for his dissimilarities as for his commonalities. She emphasized what each boy did best. She spent time with each child, but they didn't necessarily do the same things. She provided opportunities for each of them, but they weren't always the same opportunities. She monitored their growth, but she provided guidance and discipline in response to their specific needs and issues, not according to a common prescription.

Her classroom was a lot like her home. It was a given that students would differ. She found time for each child at many points during each day. She provided opportunities for everyone's growth and offered guidance as needed. The time she spent with individuals differed in format and content, and the opportunities and guidance differed according to the nature of the dreamer and the dream.

With each child, she looked for strengths and set out to find ways to fortify them. Charlie needed different art materials than some of the others. Eli needed different books to read. Sonja needed to feel the reassuring presence of the teacher to help keep her temper in tow. Michelle needed the teacher to remember to "let go" more often.

All these children were dreamers. Mary Ann and her students talked about how they were growing. They also spoke of how Mary Ann was proud of each one for his or her particular growth toward a dream. It was fine that Micah read more than the others, that Philip wiggled and moved around the classroom more, that Chauncie asked unusual questions, that Bess worked first with cubes and then with numbers, that Jorge sometimes asked his questions in Spanish first, then in English.

Mary Ann's room was big in heart, options, and support. It was big on standards, but it was short on standardization. And the 8-year-olds understood that just fine. They were not standardized people. They knew it, and they liked themselves and one another better for that.

The Content in a Healthy Classroom

A teacher once told me a story about how she came to know what and how to teach in her science class. She had wrestled with curriculum guides that were too long, texts that were too dense or too simple, labs that were sometimes fun but not illuminating, and labs that were neither illuminating nor fun. She watched her students drift away too often, and she felt smothered by what she perceived to be immutable mandates.

A colleague said to her, "Forget all the books and manuals for a minute. Go back to what it was that used to make science magic for you. Think about what it used to feel like to *do* science. Then assume the kids you teach will only have your class to learn about science. It's their only science class—ever. What do you need to teach them so they will love science? Think about that for a minute. Then change one part of what I just asked you to do. Assume you only have three kids to teach: your own three children. And assume that at the end of the year, you will die. What would you teach them about science in that year?"

The teacher said to me, "I've understood what I have to do ever since that day. I don't always know how to do what I have to do, but knowing what I have to do has changed the way I think about what I teach."

Judy Larrick taught a group of disenchanted high school students during sixth period. The curriculum guide required that she teach "classics" that her students found inaccessible and unintelligible. Attendance was down, and Judy's spirits were just as low. Lethargy was the only commodity on the rise. Judy struggled through the year cheerleading her students and trying to inject energy into essentially dead class periods. The year ended, but Judy didn't berate her students or lament the approach of another year. She went hunting for solutions.

When September came, the curriculum guide was still in place. Sixth period was still a collection of discouraged and irascible adolescents. But as school began, Judy asked, "Anybody here ever been a victim? What does it mean to be a victim? What does it feel like? Can a victim control anything in life? What? When?" A classroom full of "victims" engaged in spirited exchanges. With their teacher, they built a concept map of "victim." Finally, Judy offered, "Want to read a book about somebody else who was a victim, to see whether things play out like you said?" The students read "Antigone" as though they were discoverers of

ultimate truth. Class attendance soared and remained high.

Seventh grade teacher Judy Schlimm reflected a similar viewpoint: "My goal as a history teacher is to help my students realize that history is not the study of dead people. It's students holding up a mirror created by the past and seeing themselves in it."

These three teachers understand the essential purpose of learning. It is not an endeavor that is marked primarily by accumulation of random data. It is something far more powerful. We are born trying to gain power over our environments. We live and die trying to figure out who we are; what life means; how to understand joy, pain, victory, and death; how we must relate to others; and why we are here. The disciplines we study—art, music, literature, mathematics, history, science, or philosophy—give us lenses that help us answer life's ultimate questions. The skills of those disciplines—reading, writing, map making, computation, or illustrating—give us power to use the understandings in meaningful ways (Phenix, 1986). Thinking and puzzling about unknowns gives us far more power than rote regurgitation of isolated names, dates, facts, and definitions.

The content in a healthy classroom is rooted in these realities. Thus, in a healthy classroom, what is taught and learned

• is relevant to students; it seems personal, familiar, connected to the world they know;

• helps students understand themselves and their lives more fully now, and will continue to do so as they grow up;

• is authentic, offering "real" history or math or art, not just exercises about the subject;

• can be used immediately for something that matters to the students; and

• makes students more powerful in the present as well as in the future.

In a healthy classroom, what is taught welcomes youngsters as reasoning members of the human family, not to a standardized test or to a trivia match. As noted scientist Lewis Thomas (1983) reflects, "Instead of presenting the body of human knowledge as a mountainous structure of coherent information capable of explaining everything about everything if only we could master all the details, we should be acknowledging that it is, in real life, still a very modest mound of puzzlements that do not fit together at all" (p. 163). When subject matter is dynamic, intellectually intriguing, and personal—when it bestows power to the learner—the "details" also become more important and memorable.

Creating a Healthy Classroom Environment

Let's assume we have a teacher who is comfortable with both of her roles as leader and learner in the classroom. She understands and responds to students' essential human needs, and she understands what her subject matter really means for students. What sorts of things would that teacher do to create an environment in which she and her students continually grow in respect and caring for one another? How would she create an environment where subject matter is a catalyst for individual and group growth and appreciation? What does this teacher do to keep the learning triangle dynamic and balanced, to create a true community of learning?

Teaching is a heuristic endeavor, not an algorithmic one. Principles of teaching guide us, but are not recipes. Following are some characteristics of teaching and learning in healthy classroom environments. They are starting points for reflection, not a complete guide. Feel free to edit the list, to revise it, to add and subtract from it as you see fit.

• **The Teacher Appreciates Each Child as an Individual:** In *The Little Prince* (Saint Exupery, 1943), a young traveler encounters a fox who asks the little boy to tame him. When the child is uncertain of the fox's meaning, the fox explains, "One only understands the things that one tames" (p. 83). He explains further that the process of taming takes a long time. "You must be very patient. . . . First you must sit down at a little distance from me. . . . I shall look at you out of the corner of my eye, and you will say nothing. Words are the source of misunderstanding. But you will sit a little closer to me every day" (p. 84). The little boy comes to understand that through "taming," we learn to see the uniqueness in the thing we tame. "It is only with the heart that one can see rightly. What is essential is invisible to the eye."

Teachers in healthy classrooms work continually to "tame" their students: to see who they really are, what makes them unique in the world. There is no such thing as a child who is unattractive. There is no such thing as a child who is "okay" without teacher intervention. The teacher "tames" all comers. Teachers in healthy classrooms also take the risk of allowing their students to know them as people. They take the risk of being "tamed" themselves.

• **The Teacher Remembers to Teach Whole Children:** The teacher understands that children have intellect, emotions, and changing physical needs. He understands that he teaches children about writing or mathematics, not that he teaches mathematics or writing to children. He knows that sometimes emotions must come before the French lesson, and sometimes the French lesson can heal the emotions. He understands that a child without self-esteem will learn little. He also knows that genuine accomplishment will produce something more potent than self-esteem: self-efficacy. He knows that what the child brings from home cannot be left outside the classroom door, and for a lesson to be truly powerful, it must go home with the child.

• **The Teacher Continues to Develop Expertise:** Genuine expertise in a subject area is not so much mastery of facts as it is the application of insights and skills. An expert historian does not answer questions at the end of a chapter; she looks for new levels of understanding about places, people, and events. A writer does not just put words on a page and follow rules of grammar. He investigates meanings in the ordinary and extraordinary stories of life.

Experts use the essential skills and understandings of their disciplines at a demanding, high-quality level. A colleague remarked to me recently that the plight of teachers is that we were taught to teach science, not to be scientists. We were taught to teach public speaking, not to be orators.

• **The Teacher Links Students and Ideas:** Poet, novelist, and historical writer Paul Fleischman (Robb, 1997) described how he hoped teachers would use his book, *Dateline: Troy*, which illustrates the events of *The Iliad* with headlines from contemporary newspapers. His comments should spark meaningful reflection among all teachers.

My real hope is that teachers will be inspired to do what the best teachers have been doing all along—making seemingly remote subjects real and relevant to their students. . . . I think that showing them meaningful links to their own lives will make real readers of them, rather than takers of tests and memorizers of facts. This applies to every subject in the curriculum. Why else did I get a D in trigonometry? I was unconvinced that mastering sines and tangents was interesting in its own right or of any practical value to me. I'm confident, however, that the right teacher could convince me (p. 41).

• **The Teacher Strives for Joyful Learning:** Both words in "joyful learning" are important. In a healthy classroom, the teacher is serious about learning. It is a human birthright to be a learner. There is little we do that is more important. Further, the teacher knows we have too little time for exploring and understanding. Thus, he focuses on what matters most about a subject and ensures that the essentials are at the core of students' experiences.

On the other hand, he knows that children are somehow programmed to respond to joy. They are still full of the energy and rhythms of young life. Moving, touching things, laughing, and telling stories are prime entry points for important skills and understandings. Thus, the teacher seeks to ensure both engagement and understanding for all learners in every lesson.

Recently, a teacher in a summer program for advanced learners left a note on my office door after her fourth day of class. It said simply, "I went for rigor and got rigor mortis." Even highly advanced learners needed joy and challenge, as they made clear to this teacher.

• **The Teacher Offers High Expectations—and Lots of Ladders:** In a healthy classroom, the teacher helps students dream big. She understands that not all of the dreams will be alike, but each student needs big dreams and concrete ways to climb to them. Thus, the teacher teaches for success. That means she knows quite clearly a child's next learning benchmarks and the scaffolding needed to get there. This may include time lines, rubrics, carefully delineated product assignments, varied working arrangements in the classroom, multiple resources, partnerships with instructional specialists, or small-group reteaching or extension.

Most young learners don't know how to grow beyond where they are today until a teacher shows the way. In a healthy classroom, the teacher plays the role of a winning coach. She provides a game plan that ensures maximum success for each student. Then she stays on the sidelines, encouraging and offering advice as students "play the game."

• **The Teacher Helps Students Make Their Own Sense of Ideas:** As learners, we seldom "repeat our way to understanding." That is, giving back information through a recitation, worksheet, or test seldom produces a learner who retains and uses ideas and information. Many teachers have seen a powerful illustration of this through their own teacher education classes. Because they had no context for what professors were telling them, they often thought the classes were pointless. Once they were teaching—and had a context for the information—they had forgotten it.

Healthy classrooms are characterized by thought, wondering, and discovery. Says elementary teacher Bob Strachota (1996):

> Unless we go through the complexities of struggle and invention, our knowledge is empty. If this is true, I cannot transfer my knowledge and experience to children whom I teach. Instead I have to find ways to help children take responsibility for

inventing their own understanding of the world and how to live in it. To do this, I have to struggle against both my training and my instincts which strongly urge me to be directive: to tell children what I know, to tell them what to do (p. 5).

• **The Teacher Shares the Teaching with Students:** Teachers in healthy classrooms continually invite their students to be a part of the teaching. They do this in a number of ways. First, these teachers make it possible for students to teach one another. They believe that each student is an effective teacher of some things some of the time, but at other times they need to be taught. Second, they engage students in conversations about class rules, schedules, and procedures. Third, they do "metacognitive teaching." That is, these teachers explain to students such things as how they plan for classes, what classroom issues they puzzle over when they go home at night, and how they chart progress. While they know their leadership role, teachers in these classrooms understand that their students come with vast amounts of tacit knowledge, a clear sense of what works in their world, and valuable insights about themselves and their peers.

• **The Teacher Clearly Strives for Student Independence:** A director of a play has a peculiar job. For weeks, she orchestrates every move made by various people in a variety of roles, from actors to support personnel. Little happens without her intervention in one way or another. When the play opens, however, the director is essentially useless. If the cast and crew still need her, she is a failure.

Teaching is, or at least ought to be, like that. Every day, the teacher should make himself increasingly useless in his students' lives. These kinds of teachers do not provide solutions when students can figure things out for themselves. They provide directions and guidelines for quality, but they leave some ambiguity, choice, and flexibility so that students have to make leaps of transfer and apply common sense. They take careful measure of how much responsibility children can manage, making sure to give them that much—and coaching for a bit more as well.

Because there are too many children in classrooms, teachers often find it easier to do things for students than to contend with the complexities of having them make independent judgments. Teachers often tell me that their 2nd, 5th, or 10th graders are "just too immature to work independently." This leaves me wondering. Can you name the classroom where virtually all students work with high degrees of independence for great chunks of the day? It's kindergarten—peopled by 5-year-olds.

• **The Teacher Uses Positive Energy and Humor:** In healthy classrooms, you hear continual talk about the importance of whatever is undertaken. There is a consistent sense of urgency about what is to be learned. It isn't a sense of hurriedness, but a sense that time and topic are valuable and to be treated as such. You see the kind of planning that's done for a promising trip. Teacher and students are full of anticipation as they calculate destinations, map routes, and adjust to new contingencies.

There is a clear expectation that everyone deals with everyone else with respect and kindness. In these places, you hear laughter. Humor and creativity are close kin. Humor stems from making unexpected and pleasurable connections, from freedom to be spontaneous, from the sense that errors can be surprisingly instructive. The humor is never sarcastic or cutting. It is the sort of laughter that

stems from the capacity to laugh with one another.

• **"Discipline" Is More Covert than Overt:** Children in every classroom need reminders about how to work and how to act. It's a necessary part of growing up to be emotionally and socially sound. In healthy classrooms, however, discipline problems are rarely cataclysmic. Students gain attention and power in positive ways. They are accepted and valued, and they know it. They are aware that the teacher not only expects great things of them, but he is their partner in working toward those goals. There is opportunity to work and learn in ways that are most comfortable to them as individuals. Clear guidelines help students know how to make appropriate decisions. Genuine effort more than likely results in genuine success.

In such environments, many of the tensions that lead to misbehavior are eliminated, or at least minimized. When there is a need to deal with a severe or recurring problem, respect for the student, desire for positive growth, and shared decision-making result in understanding and learning, not conflict between adversaries.

Teaching Isn't So Different from Life

One summer when I was a child, I found a litter of kittens tucked away in a small space behind an old garage. I nearly burst waiting for my best friend to come home so I could take her to see the wonderful thing I'd discovered. All the way to the kittens, I told her how amazing my surprise was going to be. Between my exuberance and her anticipation, our walking was a cross between toe dancing and flight. When we got to the garage, I stepped back, pointed toward the tiny space, and said, "It's your turn! You go back and see."

A healthy classroom environment feels a lot like

that experience. A teacher continues to explore for wonderful finds. Sometimes she invites individuals to share the journey with her, sometimes a small group, sometimes a whole class. Whoever she takes feels specially chosen, because there is something in the invitation that says, "You are so important that I must show you the treasures I have found!"

The anticipation for this journey is great. The pace is brisk. And then there is the point where the teacher steps back and says, "I've been there. It's your turn. You think about it your way and see what your eyes make of it. You'll know what to do." Then the teacher watches the learner learn, and in so doing the teacher becomes a learner all over again.

Good Instruction as a Basis for Differentiated Teaching

5

> The Giver flicked his hand as if brushing something
> aside. "Oh, your instructors are well trained. They know
> their scientific facts. Everyone is well trained for his job.
> It's just that . . . without the memories it's all
> meaningless."
> "Why do you and I have to hold these memories?"
> [the boy asked.]
> "It gives us wisdom," the Giver replied.
> Lois Lowry
> *The Giver*

A young teacher tried her hand at developing her first differentiated lesson plan. "Could you give it a look and see if I'm on the right track?" she asked me.

Her 4th graders were all reading the same novel. She had fashioned five tasks, which she was going to assign to students based on what she perceived to be their readiness levels. The tasks were to

- create a new jacket for the book,
- build a set for a scene in the book,
- draw one of the characters,
- rewrite the novel's ending, or
- develop a conversation between a character in this novel and one from another novel they'd read in class that year.

After I looked at the tasks, I asked a question I wish someone had insisted I answer daily in the first decade of my teaching: "What do you want each student to come away with as a result of this activity?"

She squinted and answered, "I don't understand."

I tried again: "What common insight or understanding should all kids get because they successfully complete their assigned task?"

She shook her head: "I still don't get it."

"Okay. Let me try another way." I paused. "Do you want each child to know that an author actually builds a character? Do you want them all to understand why the author took the time to write the book? Do you want them to think about how the main character's life is like their own? Just what is it that the activities should cause the students to make sense of?"

Her face flushed, and she waved her hand as if shooing away a bug. "Oh my gosh!" she exclaimed. "I thought all they were supposed to do was read the story and do something with it!"

"Hazy" Lessons

Many of us are like this novice. We entered the profession with a vague sense that students should read, listen to, or watch something. Then they should do "some sort of activity" based on it. Consider the following examples.

• A 1st grade teacher reads her children a story. Then she asks them to draw a picture of what they heard. But what should the picture portray? The story's beginning and end? How the main character looked when she was frightened by the stranger? The big tree in the barnyard?

• A 5th grade teacher talks with her students about black holes. Then she shows them a video about the topic. She asks them to write a story about black holes. To learn what? Why gravity acts as it does in black holes? To deal with issues of time? To demonstrate their understanding of the evolution of black holes?

• A 3rd grade teacher studies the Westward Movement with her students. Afterward, students build covered wagons. How does that help them understand exploration, risk, scarcity of resources, or adaptation? Is the activity about pushing frontiers forward—or about manipulating glue and scissors?

In each example, the teacher had a hazy conception of what children should gain from their experience with content. Students did "something about the story," "something about black holes," "something about Westward Movement." The activities weren't deadly dull or totally useless. Nonetheless, they present at least two problems. One is a barrier to high-quality teaching and learning. The other is a barrier to powerful differentiated instruction.

When a teacher lacks clarity about what a student should know, understand, and be able to do as a result of a lesson, the learning tasks she creates may or may not be engaging and we can almost be certain the tasks won't help students understand essential ideas or principles. A fuzzy sense of the essentials results in fuzzy activities, which, in turn, results in fuzzy student understanding. That's a barrier to high-quality teaching and learning.

This kind of situation also works against differentiated instruction. With many differentiated lessons, all students need to understand the same essential principles and even use the same key skills. Yet because of variance in student readiness, interest, or learning profile, children must "come at" the ideas and use the skills in different ways. If a teacher isn't clear about what all students should understand and be able to do when the learning experience ends, he or she lacks the vital organizer around which to develop a powerful lesson. That was the problem for the novice 4th grade teacher and her five "differentiated" activities. She just created five "somethings about the novel." The activities probably would result in five fuzzy understandings about the book—or no under-standing at all.

Creating one version of an activity or product takes time. Creating two or three—and especially five!—is more labor intensive. It makes sense to ensure that you have a firm grasp of what makes a solid, powerful lesson before you create multiple versions of it. This chapter will help reduce the fuzziness that pervades much instruction. It also sets the stage for the many samples of differenti-ated instruction in the remainder of the book. Its goal is to help you fashion a sturdy foundation for differentiated instruction.

Two Essentials for Durable Learning

Over the years, I've been fascinated by students' savvy about what goes on in classrooms. I have had young adolescents say to me with diagnostic precision, "Her class is lots of fun. We don't learn a whole lot, but it's a fun class." Students understand the opposite situation, too: "We're learning math, I suppose, but it always seems like an awfully long class period."

These students voice an implicit understanding that two elements are required for a great class: engagement and understanding. Engagement hap-pens when a lesson captures students' imagina-tions, snares their curiosity, ignites their opinions, or taps into their souls. Engagement is the magnet that attracts learners' meandering attention and holds it so that enduring learning can occur.

Understanding means much more than recall-ing. It means the learner has "wrapped around" an important idea, has incorporated it accurately into his or her inventory of how things work. The learner owns the idea.

A student who understands something can

- explain it clearly, giving examples;
- use it;
- compare and contrast it with other concepts;
- relate it to other instances in the subject stud-ies, other subjects, and personal life experiences;
- transfer it to unfamiliar settings;
- discover the concept embedded within a novel problem;
- combine it appropriately with other understandings;
- pose new problems that exemplify or embody the concept;
- create analogies, models, metaphors, symbols, or pictures of the concept;
- pose and answer "what-if" questions that alter variables in a problematic situation;
- generate questions and hypotheses that lead to new knowledge and further inquiries;
- generalize from specifics to form a concept;
- use the knowledge to appropriately assess his or her own performance, or that of someone else (adapted from Barell, 1995).

Lessons that are not engaging let students' minds wander. They fail to make the case for rele-vance because students don't connect them to what's important in their lives. These kinds of les-sons have little staying power. Thus, the learner has little long-term use for unengaging lessons.

Levels of Learning

Hilda Taba (in Schiever, 1991) understood before many others that learning has several dimensions. We can learn *facts*, or discrete bits of information that we believe to be true. We can develop *concepts*, or categories of things with com-mon elements that help us organize, retain, and use information. We can understand *principles*, which are the rules that govern concepts. We develop *attitudes*, or degrees of commitment to ideas and spheres of learning. And, if we are fortunate, we develop *skills*, which are the capacity to put to work the understandings we have gained.

Full, whole, and rich learning involves all these levels. Facts without concepts and principles to promote meaning are ephemeral. Meaning without skills needed to translate them into action lose their potency. Positive attitudes about the magic of learning are stillborn until we know, understand, and can take action in our world.

Joan Bauer, author of the young adult novel *Sticks* (Bauer, 1996), speaks of the need for children and adolescents to see connectedness in learning. They need to understand that the principles of science, math, history, and art are the same ones that we find in a pool hall, in our fears, and in the deep wellsprings of courage that make us taller than our nightmares (personal communication, 1997).

In *Sticks*, Bauer displays the skill of a master teacher orchestrating all the levels of learning. She writes of 10-year-old Mickey, who has a fire in his belly to win the 10- to 13-year-olds' nine-ball championship in his grandmother's pool hall. Mickey's father was a pool champ, but he died when Mickey was a baby.

Mickey's friend, Arlen, is as passionate about math as Mickey is about nine ball. Arlen hasn't memorized math. He thinks math. It is a way of life for him. Math, he explains, will never let you down in this world. Arlen knows what an angle is. He knows that a vector is "a line that takes you from one place to another" (Bauer, 1996, p. 37). These are *facts* Arlen has learned. Yet he understands the *concepts* of energy and motion and the *principles* that govern the concepts. "Every body

remains in a state of rest or uniform motion in a straight line, unless acted on by forces from the outside. In pool talk, this means a pool ball isn't going anywhere unless it's hit by something, and once it starts moving, it needs something to stop it, like a rail, another ball, or the friction of the cloth on the table" (Bauer, 1996, p. 177).

Because Arlen sees the utility of math, his *attitude* about math is that it's a language without which many things can't be properly explained. To him, the universe is written in the language of mathematics. What matters most about Arlen, however, is not what he has learned, and not even what he understands. What matters most is his *skill*. He uses pink yarn to teach Mickey about bank shots and geometric angles, about angles of incidence and angles of reflection. "When you hit the eight ball at a certain angle to the rail, it will bound off the rail at the same angle" (Bauer, 1996, p. 179). Arlen draws diagrams of pool shots so that Mickey sees the lines his balls will draw on the table, but Mickey comes to see much more.

Mickey reflects: "In school I keep seeing the table. Long shots. Short shots. Bank shots. Vectors. I'm seeing geometry everywhere—diamond shaped ball fields, birds flying in V formation. I have grapes for lunch and think about circles. Then I ram the grapes across my tray with my straw. Wham! Two grapes in the corner. It's all connected" (Bauer, 1996, p. 141).

Arlen knew some data. What gave him power, however, was not so much what he knew (facts), but what he understood (concepts and principles) and how he could parlay his understanding into action (skills) in a situation far removed from a schoolhouse worksheet.

All subjects are built upon essential concepts and principles. All subjects, by their nature, call for use of key skills, which professionals in that field use. Some concepts are generic and cut across subjects naturally and invite linkages. Examples of generic concepts are patterns, change, interdependence, perspective, part and whole, and systems. Those concepts work well in physical education, literature, science, computer science—virtually all areas of study. Other concepts are more subject specific: They are essential to one or more disciplines, but they are not as powerful in others. Examples of subject specific concepts are probability in math, composition in art, voice in literature, structure and function in science, and primary source in history.

Similarly, skills can be generic or subject specific. Generic skills include writing a cohesive paragraph, arranging ideas in order, and posing effective questions. Skills that are subject specific include balancing an equation in math, transposing in music, using metaphorical language in literature and writing, and synthesis of sources in history. Figure 5.1 illustrates the key levels of learning in several subject areas.

During planning, a teacher should generate specific lists of what students should know (facts), understand (concepts and principles), and be able to do (skills) by the time the unit ends. Then the teacher should create a core of engaging activities that offer varied opportunities for learning the essentials she has outlined. These activities should lead a student to understand or make sense of key concepts and principles by using key skills. In later chapters of this book, illustrations of differentiated lessons typically are based on specific concepts, principles, and skills that ensure this kind of clarity.

Where Do Standards Fit In?

In many districts, teachers feel great pressure to ensure that students attain standards delineated by the district, the state, or a professional group. Standards should be a vehicle to ensure that students learn more coherently, more deeply, more broadly, and more durably. Sadly, when teachers feel pressure to "cover" standards in isolation, and when the standards are presented in the form of fragmented and sterile lists, genuine learning is hobbled, not enriched.

Each standard in a prescribed list is either a fact, concept, principle, attitude, or skill. It is a valuable exercise for teachers, administrators, and curriculum specialists to examine standards lists, labeling each standard with its level of learning.

Some sets of standards are based on concepts and principles, integrating skills of the particular discipline into networks of understanding. That is the case with many of the standards developed by national professional groups. In other instances, however, standards reflect predominately skill-level learning, with an occasional attitude level, and less frequently a principle level. When this is the case, educators need to "fill in the blanks," making certain that learning experiences are solidly based on concepts and principles and that students use skills in meaningful ways to achieve or act upon meaningful ideas.

This point hit home for me when I recently heard one educator telling another about a classroom she had visited. "I asked the child what the class was working on," the educator reported. "She told me they were writing paragraphs, and I asked what they were writing about. She told me again they were writing paragraphs, and I smiled and asked, 'But *why* are you writing the paragraphs?

Figure 5.1
Examples of the Levels of Learning

Levels of Learning	Science	Literature	History	Music	Math	Art	Reading
Facts	Water boils at 212° C. Humans are mammals.	Katherine Paterson wrote *Bridge to Terebithia*. Definition of plot and definition of character.	The Boston Tea Party helped to provoke the American Revolution. The first 10 amendments to the U.S. Constitution are called the Bill of Rights.	Strauss was The Waltz King. Definition of clef.	Definition of numerator and denominator. Definition of prime numbers.	Monet was an Impressionist. Definition of primary colors.	Definition of vowel and consonant.
Concepts	Interdependence. Classification	Voice. Heroes and antiheroes	Revolution. Power, authority, and governance	Tempo. Jazz	Part and whole. Number systems	Perspective. Negative space	Main idea. Context
Principles	All life forms are part of a food chain. Scientists classify animals according to patterns.	Authors use voices of characters as a way of sharing their own voices. Heroes are born of danger or uncertainty.	Revolutions are first evolutions. Liberty is constrained in all societies.	The tempo of a piece of music helps to set the mood. Jazz is both structured and improvisational.	Wholes are made up of parts. The parts of a number system are interdependent.	Objects can be viewed and represented from a variety of perspectives. Negative space helps spotlight essential elements in a composition.	Effective paragraphs generally present and support a main idea. Pictures and sentences often help us figure out words we don't know.
Attitudes	Conservation benefits our ecosystem. I am part of an important natural network.	Reading poetry is boring. Stories help me understand myself.	It's important to study history so we write the next chapters more wisely. Sometimes I am willing to give up some freedom to protect the welfare of others.	Music helps me to express emotion. I don't care for jazz.	Math is too hard. Math is a way of talking about lots of things in my world.	I prefer Realism to Impressionism. Art helps me to see the world better.	I am a good reader. It's hard to "read between the lines."
Skills	Creating a plan for an energy efficient school. Interpreting data about costs and benefits of recycling.	Using metaphorical language to establish personal voice. Linking heroes and antiheroes in literature with those of history and current life.	Constructing and supporting a position on an issue. Drawing conclusions based on analyses of sound resources.	Selecting a piece of music that conveys a particular emotion. Writing an original jazz composition.	Expressing parts and wholes in music and the stock market, with fractions and decimals. Showing relationships among elements.	Responding to a painting with both affective and cognitive awareness. Presenting realistic and impressionistic views of an object.	Locating main idea and supporting details in news articles. Interpreting themes in stories.

What are you trying to communicate?' She answered me with some irritation, 'Oh, that doesn't matter. We're just writing paragraphs!'"

Put another way, teaching skills without coherent, meaning-rich ideas is hollow. In addition, teaching mechanics without meaning is counter to the way humans learn (as was discussed in Chapter 3).

Learning Levels: A Case in Point

I once watched two 3rd grade teachers scramble to figure out how they could "cover" another unit in science before the year ended. They told me they had "moved too slowly." They still had to "do clouds" with students in the few remaining days of class.

The two teachers worked hard to lay out materials from science books, which they would have their students read. They found some stories about clouds that students usually liked, hoping they'd have time to read them. The two teachers agreed on cloud worksheets the students could complete, and they chose an art activity the students would enjoy. All this work seemed very urgent and purposeful. Yet as the two began to decide the order in which they'd use the materials, one teacher discovered she had forgotten the name of one kind of cloud. The second teacher realized she recalled the names, but she couldn't match the names to any pictures. Both teachers had "taught the cloud unit" several times.

This example of "planning a unit" is common. With good intent, teachers try to do what their program of study outlines. In this case, the outline said students should know and recognize the kinds of clouds. While the curriculum guide may state how this segment of study fits into a larger

framework of understandings and skills, the guide did not make that explicit to the teachers who, in turn, would not make it explicit to their students. Thus, the "unit" these teachers prepared was largely fact-based and devoid of concepts, principles, and skills. Not surprisingly, even the teachers who had taught the unit for several years had difficulty recalling the facts. This did not portend rich, long-term outcomes for the students!

By contrast, another teacher mapped out her whole year in science around four key concepts: change, patterns, systems, and interrelationships. All year, students examined a range of scientific phenomena, learning how they illustrated the four concepts. At the outset of each exploration, the teacher developed essential principles she wanted all students to come to understand through their study. Some of the principles were repeated in several units. (For example: Natural and human made things change over time. Change in one part of a system affects other parts of the system. We can use patterns to make intelligent predictions.) Some generalizations were specific to a particular study. (For example: Water can change in form. Living things are part of ecosystems.)

The teacher also created a list of skills students were to master in the course of the year. For example, her students needed to learn to use particular weather tools, to make predictions based on observations rather than guesses, and to communicate data through pictures and written statements. The teacher chose appropriate places in the various studies to have students use the skills to understand key principles. Facts were everywhere as students talked about specific events just as scientists would.

At one point in the year, students used weather instruments (skills) to talk about patterns and interrelationships in weather systems (concepts). They explored two principles: (1) that change in one part of a system affects other parts of the system and (2) we can use patterns to make intelligent predictions. Then they predicted (skill) what sorts of clouds (facts) would be likely to form as a result of the patterns and interrelationships they saw. They illustrated and wrote about their predictions using appropriate cloud terminology. They then observed what happened, assessed the accuracy of their predictions, and communicated their observations in the form of revised drawings and explanations.

This kind of planning for student learning creates a structure for coherent understanding all year. Facts illustrate and cement key ideas that are rediscovered repeatedly. Skills have a purpose rooted in meaning and utility. The learning promotes both engagement and understanding. These students are more likely to understand how their world works and to feel more competent as learners and young scientists. They also are more likely to remember the names and nature of clouds a year or two down the road—and so is their teacher!

Curriculum Elements

To ensure effective teaching and learning, remember that teachers need to link tightly three key elements of curriculum: content, process, and product. (The other two elements of curriculum are learning environment and affect. Those elements were introduced in Chapter 3, and they must consistently remain central to thinking about, planning for, observing, and assessing instruction.)

Content is what a student should come to know (facts), understand (concepts and principles), and

be able to do (skills) as a result of a given segment of study (a lesson, a learning experience, a unit). Content is "input." It encompasses the means by which students will become acquainted with information (through textbooks, supplementary readings, videos, field trips, speakers, demonstrations, lectures, or computer programs).

Process is the opportunity for students to make sense of the content. If we only tell students something and then ask them to tell it back to us, they are highly unlikely to incorporate it into their frameworks of understanding. The information and ideas will belong to someone else (teacher, textbook writer, speaker). Students must process the ideas to own them. In the classroom, process typically takes place in the form of activities. An activity is likely to be effective if it

• has a clearly defined instructional purpose,

• focuses students squarely on one key understanding,

• causes students to use a key skill to work with key ideas,

• ensures that students will have to understand (not just repeat) the idea,

• helps students relate new understandings and skills to previous ones, and

• matches the student's level of readiness.

A product is a vehicle through which a student shows (and extends) what he or she has come to understand and can do as a result of a considerable segment of learning (such as a month-long study of mythology, a unit on weather systems, a marking period spent on studying governments, a semester learning to speak French, or a year spent investigating ecosystems). The examples in this book use the term "product" to mean "culminating product," or something students produce to exhibit major portions of learning. It is not used to talk about pieces of work students produce during the course of a day. For the purposes of this book, those short-term creations simply are concrete and visible elements of an activity.

A culminating product might take the form of a demonstration or exhibition. Students could design a solution to a complex problem or undertake major research and writing. A culminating product could be a test, or it could be a visual display, such as a narrated photo essay.

An effective assignment for a culminating product will:

• Clearly lay out what students should demonstrate, transfer, or apply to show what they understand and can do as a result of the study.

• Provide one or more modes of expression.

• Lay out clear, precise expectations for high-quality content (information, ideas, concepts, research sources); steps and behaviors of developing the product (planning, effective use of time, goal setting, originality, insight, editing); and the nature of the product itself (size, audience, construction, durability, format, delivery, mechanical accuracy).

• Provide support and scaffolding for high-quality student success. (For example, provide opportunities to brainstorm ideas, delineate rubrics, and establish time lines. Conduct in-class workshops on use of research materials, or provide opportunities for peer critiques and peer editing.)

• Provide for variations in student readiness, interest, and learning profile.

Joining Learning Levels and Curriculum

A top-rate teacher is clear about all levels of learning in whatever unit or segment she is exploring with her students. She then makes certain that

content, process, and product are built around materials and experiences that lead students to engage with and genuinely understand the subject. That means content, process, and product are squarely focused on exploring and mastering key concepts, essential principles, related skills, and necessary facts (see Figure 5.2). The following example illustrates how this sort of thinking and planning might look.

Ms. Johnson and her middle schoolers are beginning a study of mythology. The concepts she and her students will explore in this study (and throughout the year) include hero, voice, culture, and identity. Among the principles they will investigate are the following:

• People tell stories to clarify their beliefs for themselves and for others.

• Our stories reflect our culture.

• Understanding someone else's view of the world helps us clarify our own view.

• When we compare the unfamiliar with the familiar, we understand both better.

• Who a person, or culture, designates as hero tells much about the person or culture.

• Myths are mirrors of values, religion, family, community, science, and reasoning.

Among skills that will be emphasized in the month-long study: paragraphing, punctuating dialogue, comparison and contrast, and interpreting and using similes and metaphors. As is the case throughout the year, the teacher makes certain students use the vocabulary of fiction (plot, setting, protagonist, theme, tone) as they talk about and work with the myths. She also ensures that students encounter characters and events (facts) from key myths often and in various contexts. This way they become familiar with important names and events that contribute to the vocabulary,

Figure 5.2
Joining Levels of Learning and Elements of Curriculum

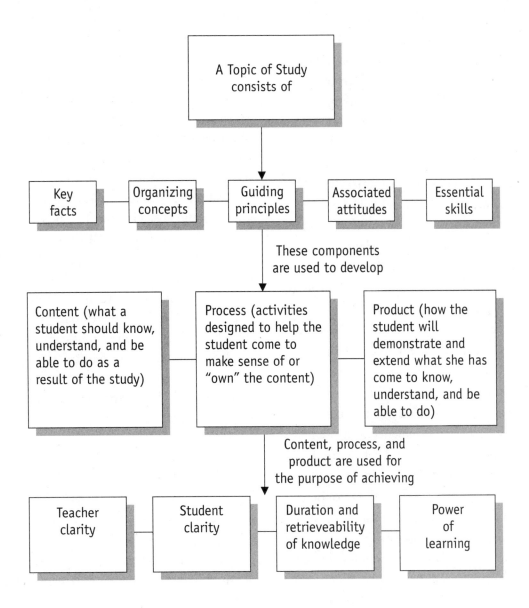

symbols, and allusions throughout their own and other cultures.

Knowing the key facts, concepts, and principles she intends her students to learn directs Ms. Johnson's selection of myths (content). She knows, for example, that she must select myths that reflect several cultures; include clear exemplars of heroes; reveal views about religion, community, and science; and introduce events and characters that are the basis for oft-used cultural symbols and allusions.

Ms. Johnson develops core activities that help students link what they read and talk about from the myths with their own cultures, beliefs, and ways of thinking. Further, she develops activities so students must use targeted skills to complete them, and she directly teaches the skills as the students need them. For example, she and the students will decide what makes a hero in Greek, Norse, and African myths. She's considering having students write, and perhaps present, a conversation between a mythological hero and a contemporary hero. She'll ask the students to do this in a way that lets the audience compare and contrast the heroes' cultures and beliefs. To do this, students will have to know important characters and events, understand the concept of hero, apply the principles they've been studying, and use the skill of punctuating dialogue.

When she develops an assignment for a culminating product, Ms. Johnson offers several options. However, all the options require students to

- demonstrate their understanding of myths as mirrors of hero and culture;
- use core knowledge about important characters and events from important myths; and
- use the targeted skills of metaphorical thought and language, punctuation of dialogue, and comparison and contrast.

Ms. Johnson's clarity about what students must know, understand, and be able to do as a result of a unit promotes engagement. Students see ancient myths as very much like their own lives. The myths make sense, seem real, and connect to things they feel are important. The myths promote understanding because they link new knowledge and insight with the familiar.

Ms. Johnson's activities help students build frameworks to organize and think about knowledge and ideas. They provide reinforcing and connective learning opportunities through all elements of the curriculum. Ms. Johnson has not yet started to think about differentiating instruction for varied student readiness, interest, and learning profile. However, she is laying the foundation for doing so in a rich and meaningful way.

For More Information

For additional information about concept-based teaching and alignment with learning standards see the following resource.

Erikson, H. (1998). *Concept-based curriculum and instruction: Teaching beyond the facts*. Thousand Oaks, CA: Corwin.

Teachers at Work Building Differentiated Classrooms

6

> These teachers were well experienced with traditional
> ways of schooling. . . . But they also wanted much more.
> They wanted to do studies that would be likely to win
> genuine commitments from their kids, studies that would
> offer so many options that each student could work "at
> his or her own level." In brief, they were ready for serious
> curriculum innovation—to explore some compelling
> possibilities that would extend them and their students.
> Chris Stevenson & Judy Carr, Editors
> *Integrated Studies in the Middle Grades:*
> *Dancing Through Walls*

Teachers in the most exciting and effective differentiated classes don't have all the answers. Instead, they are dogged learners who come to school every day with the conviction that today will reveal a better way of doing things—even if yesterday's lesson was dynamite. They believe they can find this better way if only they aggressively search out and examine the clues implicit in what they do. This conviction guides all aspects of their work, every single day.

These kinds of teachers shun "recipe" teaching. They know that even if they do filch an idea from someone else's store of ideas (a time-honored and defensible practice among teachers!), they must adapt it for their own learners' needs, fit it to essential learning goals in their own classroom, and polish it so it becomes a catalyst for engagement and understanding among their own students. Long-time teacher Susan Ohanian (1988) expands on this point. She draws on Confucius's admonition that someone can reveal to us "one corner" of understanding, but we must find the other three ourselves.

> I know plenty of teachers who are
> disappointed, indignant, and eventually
> destroyed by the fact that nobody has
> handed them all four corners. . . . It is up to
> us to read the research and to collaborate

with the children to find the other three corners. And because teaching must be a renewable contract, if we don't keep seeking new understanding, we'll find that the corners we thought we knew very well will keep slipping away. There are constant, subtle shifts in the schoolroom. One can never be sure of knowing the floor plan forever and ever (Ohanian, 1988, p. 60).

Chapters 6, 7, and 8 offer examples of differentiated curriculum and instruction to illustrate key principles of differentiation (see Figure 6.1). These are not ready-made lessons to be transported into other classrooms. Instead, these lessons reveal "one corner" of the differentiation process to start other teachers in pursuit of "the other three."

The annotations that accompany these examples are as valuable as the illustrations themselves, if not more so. They illuminate the thought processes, or the heuristics, that will enable teachers to search for the "other three corners" with their particular students, in their particular subject areas, and according to their particular personalities and needs as educators and human beings.

Differentiating: What, How, and Why

When thinking about differentiated curriculum and instruction, three questions are useful for analysis: What is the teacher differentiating? How is she differentiating? Why is she differentiating?

In the examples given in the sections that follow, **Differentiate What** refers to the curricular element the teacher has modified in response to learner needs. That is, it illustrates the teacher modifying

• content (what students will learn and the materials that represent that),

• process (activities through which students make sense of key ideas using essential skills),

• product (how students demonstrate and extend what they understand and can do as a result of a span of learning), or

• learning environment (the classroom conditions that set the tone and expectations of learning).

One or more of these elements can be modified for any given learning experience.

Differentiate How refers to the student trait to which the differentiation responds. It shows how the teacher differentiates in response to student readiness, interest, or learning profile. Again, any

---

Figure 6.1
Key Principles of a Differentiated Classroom

The teacher is clear about what matters in subject matter.

The teacher understands, appreciates, and builds upon student differences.

Assessment and instruction are inseparable.

The teacher adjusts content, process, and product in response to student readiness, interests, and learning profile.

All students participate in respectful work.

Students and teachers are collaborators in learning.

Goals of a differentiated classroom are maximum growth and individual success.

Flexibility is the hallmark of a differentiated classroom.

learning experience can be modified to respond to one or more of these traits.

Differentiate Why addresses the teacher's reason for modifying the learning experience. Teachers believe modification is important for many reasons. Three key reasons include access to learning, motivation to learn, and efficiency of learning. Any or all of these three reasons for differentiating instruction can be tied to student readiness, interest, and learning profile.

For example, we can't learn that which is inaccessible to us because we don't understand it. We can't learn when we are unmotivated by things that are far too difficult—or too easy—for us. We learn more enthusiastically those things that connect to our interests, and we learn more efficiently if we have a suitable background of experience. We also learn more efficiently if we can acquire information and express our understanding through a preferred mode.

The following sections present examples of differentiated curriculum and instruction. Some of them reflect modest, though important, modifications. Others are more elaborate. Each section is followed by an analysis of what the teacher was thinking as he planned in response to student needs. You might find it interesting to do your own analysis before reading the one provided.

Differentiation and Skills-Focused Instruction

Consistently teaching skills in isolation can strip learning of relevance and power. Yet there are times in most classes when teachers appropriately opt to have students practice a specific skill. In best-case scenarios, teachers then ask students to complete meaning-rich tasks or knotty problems using the skills.

In any class, student readiness for particular skills is often varied. Thus, most teachers see an acute need to differentiate how students practice skills. Here are some examples of teachers differentiating skills-focused assignments based on their assessment and understanding of students' points of entry.

Grade 1: Classification

Yesterday, Mrs. Lane's 1st graders took a nature walk to gather objects they could think about as scientists might. Today, they will work in groups to classify the items they found on their walk.

All students will first classify items as living or nonliving. Then, within those categories, students will classify by other similarities (such as shape, size, color, and type of object). Mrs. Lane has made one adaptation at several tables. Some of the early 1st graders will classify only the actual objects. At other tables, she has replaced some of the objects with cards that bear the object's name. This is for early readers excited about their newly evolving skill. Based on their readiness to decode the object names, several of the early readers have one or two cards, but others have many.

Differentiate What: The teacher is differentiating materials. Therefore, she is differentiating the content.

Differentiate How: She is modifying instruction based on her ongoing assessment of students' reading readiness.

Differentiate Why: She wants young readers to have as many chances as possible to use their reading skills. The word cards help nonreaders, too. When students at the various tables share how they classified the items, the nonreaders will encounter examples of object-word connection, which is essential to learning to read.

Grade 4: Proofreading Center

Fourth graders in Mr. Mack's class go to a center where they refine their ability to detect and correct errors in punctuation, spelling, and sentence structure. Sometimes they find written messages from characters in stories they are reading, people in current events, their teacher, or the gnomes and trolls Mr. Mack declares inhabit the classroom's crannies to observe what goes on. Mr. Mack, of course, writes these pieces with humor, a dash of wisdom, and varying degrees and types of errors, depending on which students will be called upon to edit them.

At other times, students leave their own writing in an in-box at the proofreading center so peers can help them polish their drafts. Mr. Mack screens these pieces, too, asking particular students to review certain papers, which he knows they can respond to in a meaningful way based on the author's needs and the reviewer's proficiency.

Differentiate What: Skills-based content is the focus of teacher assessment. Mr. Mack then differentiates the process or activities he crafts to be a good match for students' skill needs.

Differentiate How: The teacher is predominately differentiating based on readiness, which, in this case, is proficiency in spelling, punctuation, and sentence structure. He's also keenly aware of student interests. He has a great time dashing off error-ridden notes from book characters, sports heroes, or gnomes, knowing these notes will strike a chord with particular learners. He also matches topics of student writing with reviewer interest

whenever he can. The approach works. Students look forward to proofreading in Mr. Mack's class.

Differentiate Why: Mr. Mack's students have different skill needs in writing and proofing. Thus, varying the errors provides him with an efficient way to move students along the skills continuum as quickly as possible. He also avoids undue boredom from unnecessary repetition of previously mastered skills, and he circumvents the confusion that occurs when the skills called for are beyond a student's readiness. His awareness of student readiness also allows him to convene various small groups for direct instruction on particular skills, and he can bring together groups with similar tasks for the purpose of checking work. Further, his students are highly motivated by his humor and the chance to help a peer do better with writing.

Grade 2: Alphabetizing

Ms. Howe built several alphabetizing boards with the heads of large nails protruding from brightly colored plywood. Students practice their alphabetizing skills by hanging words on the nails in appropriate order.

Ms. Howe gives a student a cup of round, paper key tags with metal rims. Each tag has a word to be alphabetized. Some cups contain unfamiliar words with few syllables and distinctly different initial letters. Others contain words that closely resemble one another in spelling or configuration. Sometimes she puts a made-up word on a tag. Students get a small treat if they spot the phoney word and "prove" to the class why it's fake by citing a rule or using a dictionary as evidence.

Differentiate What: The activity, or process, stays essentially the same. It's the material, or content, that varies.

Differentiate How: Again, skills readiness is the focus of differentiation. For one student, ordering words like "car" and "cap" is a considerable challenge. For others, words like "choose" and "chose" or "library" and "librarian" are more appropriately challenging.

Differentiate Why: Here, too, efficiency of learning and access to understanding are important to the teacher. She is trying to meet each student where her skills currently are, and she wants to help each child move on as rapidly as possible. It's important to remember that one set of materials may have a long lifespan. A cup of tags that challenges a grade-level reader in September may be just right in December for a student whose skills are developing more slowly.

Grade 8: Physical Education

Many times, Mr. Grant organizes whole-class volleyball games in his physical education classes so students can learn to function as a team. At other times, he divides the class in half. At one end of the gym, students play a volleyball game. Mr. Grant asks different students to referee these games: students with leadership skills and students who are comfortable with the sport. At the other end of the gym, he assembles a group of students needing work with a common skill, such as setting the ball, spiking the ball, or receiving the ball without shrinking from it. Students in the groups for direct instruction vary often and widely.

Differentiate What: Mr. Grant is differentiating the opportunity students have to develop mastery of a skill. Both the particular skill (content) and the small-group activity (process) vary.

Differentiate How: In large measure, he is focusing on student readiness in a skill. He also

may be attending to student learning profile when he gives students with leadership talent an opportunity to hone those skills.

Differentiate Why: Students feel better about their participation in a sport when they can develop their prowess in it. They have greater access to that opportunity when their individual needs are addressed in a systematic, focused way for at least some of the class time.

Grades 10 and 11: Foreign Language

In a skills-focused exercise for Mrs. Higgins's German 1 class, she and her students will emphasize formation of past-tense verbs. But Mrs. Higgins's students vary quite widely in speed and facility of learning a foreign language.

One group of students having difficulty with grammatical concepts in general, and German in particular, will work with pattern drills in which much of a German sentence is supplied. However, each sentence uses an English verb, and students must supply the correct form of the past-tense German verb. Occasionally, an English noun or pronoun also appears, and students must supply the correct German verb. Mrs. Higgins has ensured that the missing verbs are regular and that other missing elements are essential to basic translation and conversation.

A second, somewhat more proficient, group has a similar activity. But they will encounter a greater number and complexity of missing words, including a few irregular verbs. Another group of students works with the same sentences as the second group, but virtually all of the sentences are in English and must be translated into German. Two or three students in Mrs. Higgins's classes don't need the skill drill. They are given a scenario to develop, with instructions about the sorts of grammatical constructions that must be included. They may develop the scenario for written or taped presentation to the teacher. A task that one group completes today may become homework for a less-advanced group within the next few days.

Differentiate What: Students are working with varied content. While all of them focus on past-tense verbs, other sentence and vocabulary elements vary.

Differentiate How: Student readiness is targeted, based on proficiency in providing basic grammatical constructions.

Differentiate Why: Some students really need an additional, guided chance to practice basic, regular verb formation before moving on to other challenges. Other students are ready to grapple with the more complex and unpredictable irregular verbs. They can draw on a greater range of sentence elements and vocabulary. When she varies requirements by degrees of complexity, independence, and open-endedness, Mrs. Higgins ensures that all students escalate smoothly in skill from their current comfort levels. Having students work with readiness-appropriate tasks also enables her to better target direct instruction and monitor small groups. This process, which she uses every few days, ensures that students struggling with German don't add to their confusion and sense of failure by skipping steps of understanding. It also ensures that quick learners don't "stand still" and develop a sense of complacency with the language.

Grade 6: Spelling

Ms. Estes pretests her students on spelling in September. Typically, she finds students who work with 2nd grade words and others who top out of an 8th grade list. She uses a spelling procedure that is the same for all students, but each student works on a particular list indicated by current spelling performance. She color codes the lists rather than labeling them with grade equivalents.

Students have a spelling notebook in which they write the next 10 words from their spelling list. Students create sentences with their words, have a peer check them, correct errors, take them to the teacher for a final check, correct any remaining errors, write each word five times, then take a quiz on the 10 words, which is administered by a peer. Any words missed become part of the next list. The teacher gives individual survey tests on numerous past lists on a rotating basis. Again, misspelled words are "recycled" onto the next list. The repetitions in this procedure prove to be quite effective in helping students internalize key spelling patterns. Students who demonstrate proficiency with 8th grade words at any point in the year work with a vocabulary procedure that emphasizes root words and derivatives from a variety of languages that have contributed to the evolution of English.

Differentiate What: Ms. Estes is differentiating content by varying the spelling lists. The process or activity remains the same for all students, except those who have tested out of spelling. For them, both content and process are modified.

Differentiate How: All of the spelling differentiation is based on assessment of student readiness.

Differentiate Why: This procedure provides access to growth for all students at a rate appropriate for them individually. The independence and peer assistance are quite motivating to the middle schoolers.

Grade 7: Review in All Subjects

"Blitzball" is a big hit on the 7th grade team. A number of teachers use it to review ideas and information and to help students latch onto important knowledge and understandings.

Prompted by teacher review guides, students work in mixed-readiness groups of four to six to make sure they know and understand key information. Then the teams compete in Blitzball. The teacher calls on a student, who comes to a line made of masking tape. The teacher asks the student a question. When the student answers correctly, he earns a chance to throw a tennis ball at a brightly painted plywood backboard. It has four small holes at each corner and a large hole in the center. Hitting the board gets one point for the team. Sending the ball through the center hole nets three points. A team earns five points when the ball goes through one of the small holes.

Students in the audience who talk during the game lose five points for their team. All the students stay alert for toss-up questions and opportunities to challenge answers for points. The teacher adjusts questions based each student's level of understanding and skill. This ensures that each student is appropriately challenged and has a fair chance to gain team points.

Differentiate What: Content is differentiated; the activity remains constant.

Differentiate How: The teacher differentiates by student readiness in the particular subject at that time.

Differentiate Why: Students are highly motivated by the fast-paced game, and they are even more motivated because each student has an equal chance of earning a toss. An interesting additional motivator stems from the reality that capacity to throw a ball skillfully does not necessarily correlate with student readiness in a subject; maximum points are often earned by students who may not be academic stars.

Other Principles Reflected in the Examples

Skills-based activities are not always high on the engagement scale. But many of the teachers we've seen have been effective in making their activities user-friendly with humor, opportunities for movement, and student collaboration. In all of these instances, the activities are equally respectful in that one version doesn't look preferable to—or less desirable than—any other. The principle of equally respectful activities also is evident in that every student is squarely focused on whatever skill the teacher deems essential.

We also have seen teachers using ongoing assessment of student readiness, interest, and learning profile for the purpose of matching task to student need. They do not force-fit students to tasks. It's also clear in these examples that readiness relates to a particular competency at a particular time; it does not equate to a statement about a child's overall ability or inability.

For example, a child who is a very apt thinker in literature may have difficulty spelling. A student who spells well may have difficulty with reading comprehension. A child who has a beastly time writing German sentences may do quite well with oral language. Some students struggle with many things, and others are advanced with many things. But most have areas in which they are more fluid and some in which they are less fluid. It is fairer and more accurate to look at readiness for a particular endeavor instead of using one skill to make a judgment about general ability.

Finally, teachers in these illustrations are crafting "escalators of learning." They do not assume there is one spelling list for all 6th graders, one set of volleyball skills for all 7th graders, or one set of sentences for every novice German student. These teachers demonstrate a systematic intent to find students who are one floor—or two or three—below performance expectations and to move them up with minimal gaps and no sense of despair. There is also systematic intent to find learners who are a floor—or two or three—above performance expectations, and to move them further upward with minimal "marching in place" and a sense that learning is synonymous with striving and challenge.

Differentiation and Concept-Based Instruction

The principles and beliefs reflected in the previous section are still at work in the examples of differentiated instruction that follow. However, the next examples demonstrate a teacher's intent to integrate several or all levels of learning (facts, concepts, principles, attitudes, and skills) and to differentiate curriculum and instruction from that very rich starting point.

Grade 12: Government

Over the next three days, seniors in Mr. Yin's government class are conducting research in groups of three to five. Their goal is to understand how the Bill of Rights has expanded over time and its impact on various groups in society. Students will continue an ongoing exploration of the concept of change. They also will explore the principle that the documents and institutions that govern societies change to meet the demands of changing times. They will work with skills of research and expository writing.

Mr. Yin has placed students in groups of somewhat similar readiness (for example, struggling readers to grade-level readers, or grade-level readers to advanced readers). All research groups must examine an issue such as

• how one or more amendments in the Bill of Rights became more inclusive over time,

• societal events that prompted reinterpretation of one or more amendments in the Bill of Rights,

• court decisions that redefined one or more of the amendments,

• current interpretations and applications of one or more of the amendments, or

• unresolved issues related to the amendments.

Students also have a common rubric for the structure and content of appropriate writing, and they will be asked individually to develop a written piece that stems from what they have learned from their group's research. A wide range of print, computer, video, and audio resources are available to all groups.

Despite common elements in the assignment, Mr. Yin has differentiated the work in two important ways. Some research groups will investigate societal groups that are more familiar to them, areas where issues are more clearly defined, or areas where there is more information available on a basic reading level. Other groups will examine unfamiliar societal groups, issues that are less defined, or issues where the library resources are more complex.

Students may choose to write an essay, parody, or dialogue to reflect their understandings. The teacher will provide guidelines for each form.

Differentiate What: While questions in the activity remain constant, the activity or process varies in mode of expression. In addition, research resources, a facet of content, vary.

Differentiate How: Mr. Yin has decided to modify instruction based on students' sophistication in reading, writing, and abstract thinking. (He could have modified for interest by encouraging students to select a societal group in which they were particularly interested.) Further, his three product options address both readiness and learning profile. The essay is likely to require less complex thought and manipulation of language than the parody. Some students might be more drawn to the dialogue format than to the essay format.

Differentiate Why: Mr. Yin sees access to materials as an important issue. Research materials differ greatly in complexity, and issues can differ greatly in clarity. By matching students to materials and issues, he maximizes the likelihood that students will come away appropriately challenged. They also will have a grasp of essential concepts and principles. Similarly, he has provided options for expression at varying degrees of difficulty. The fact that he has made some choices for the three days and encouraged students to make others balances the teacher's role as diagnostician with students' needs to make decisions about their own learning.

Grade 1: Patterns

Mr. Morgan and his 1st graders look for patterns in language, art, music, science, and numbers—everywhere they go. They understand the principles that patterns use repetition and that patterns are predictable. Today Mr. Morgan and his students are working with patterns in writing.

As a whole class, they have looked at how writers like Dr. Seuss use language patterns. They've clapped out the patterns together; recited them; and talked about sounds, words, and sentences. They have listened to their teacher read part of a pattern in a book, and they have predicted what would come next.

Mr. Morgan just read his students *The Important Book* by Margaret Wise Brown (1949), which also uses patterns. The pattern it uses is as follows:

> The important thing about _____ is that it is _____ . It is _____ . It is _____ . And it is _____ . But the important thing about _____ is that it is _____ .
>
> For example: The important thing about night is that it is dark. It is quiet. It is creepy. And it is scary. But the important thing about night is that it is dark.

Now the 1st graders are going to make an "Important" book for their class, showing how they can use writing patterns. Mr. Morgan will have them work in groups of varying sizes to write the pages. Some students will work with him to select the important object they will write about. These students need more assistance with the concept of a pattern and with writing itself. He will guide them as they tell him what to write on chart paper, making sure they work together to select a topic, describe what's important about it, and complete the pattern. He also will have them take turns reading their page, individually and as a group, and he will have each student talk about the repetition in the pattern and how it is predictable. Once the chart page is completed, Mr. Morgan will convert it into a book-sized page that matches others being created in the class.

Some students will work in pairs to complete a "template" page that Mr. Morgan has created.

They will select their own language to complete the template and do the writing themselves. However, Mr. Morgan has given these students a list of nouns and adjectives from which they can draw if they "get stuck." A few students in the class are very advanced with writing. Their job is to create a page for the book "from scratch." They may refer to the original book if they need to, but most will develop the page from memory and can manage the writing adequately on their own.

Mr. Morgan will ask students from all working groups to read their pages to the class at some time over the next few days. He'll use this opportunity to have students talk about what a pattern is and how patterns are used in their book. Ultimately, students will illustrate the book pages, make a cover and title page (which are examples of patterns in books), bind the book, and add it to a growing collection of books about patterns they have created for their class library.

Differentiate What: Content in this scenario stays basically the same. All students are working with the same concept and principles, and all are working with skills of writing. The activity or process varies as the teacher adds or withdraws support and guidance in making the book pages.

Differentiate How: Based on his assessment of student independence in writing and developing patterns, the teacher differentiated the activity in response to student readiness.

Differentiate Why: In most 1st grade classes, students demonstrate a wide range of language skills. In this case, all students needed a chance to explore patterns, recognize patterns, contribute to pattern formation, work with writing skills, and contribute to the class book. However, to be appropriately challenging for the full span of language development, the writing task had to be presented at varying degrees of structure. It also called on varied stages of language development.

Grade 9: U.S. History

The following extended example describes how Mrs. Lupold and her 9th graders studied the Industrial Revolution in the United States. She has developed a concept-based unit that attends to student commonalities as well as their differences in readiness, interest, and learning profile. The example provides a clear illustration of a teacher attending to student readiness, interest, and learning profile. It also reflects key principles of differentiation, such as use of flexible grouping and ensuring respectful assignments for all learners.

This unit (and others throughout the year) is based on ideas such as interdependence, change, revolution, and scarcity versus plenty. Students will examine principles such as:

• Changes in one part of a society affect other parts of the society as well.

• People resist change.

• Change is necessary for progress.

• When members of a society have uneven access to economic resources, conflict often arises.

• The struggles of one historical period are much like those of other historical periods.

Among skills emphasized are comprehension of text materials, note taking, analysis, and identification and transfer of historical themes.

Without telling students the name of the "new" time period they are about to study, Mrs. Lupold asks students to work with classmates at their tables (random seating) to create a web or mind map of what was going on in history as their previous unit concluded. This helps them use what they already have learned to build a foundation for what is to come.

She invites students who like to read aloud to volunteer to take home excerpts from two novels. They can practice reading aloud so they will be prepared to read for the class the next day. She offers students who have difficulty reading selections from *Lyddie* by Katherine Paterson (1991). These passages are manageable by most students with below-grade reading skills. She offers stronger readers passages from *The Dollmaker* by Harriett Arnow (1954), a book for adult-level readers.

The next day, volunteers read powerful passages from the two novels. The passages describe living conditions during the Industrial Revolution in the United States, though they do not name it as such. Mrs. Lupold then asks students to do a "Think-Pair-Share-Square" on this question: "What could possibly be going on in our country to have people living this way?" Students first write their ideas for two minutes. They then turn to a thinking partner of their choice (someone close so no walking is involved). They discuss their thoughts for two minutes, then each pair is joined by another pair for a four-way exchange. They discuss the question for two more minutes, then the teacher poses the question again for whole-class discussion.

Eventually she helps them link what they heard in the novels with the webs they drew the day before. She tells them the new period is called the Industrial Revolution, and she helps them speculate how that name predicts what will happen in the novels. They end class by creating a chart. The teacher lists the things students know about the Industrial Revolution, things they think they know but aren't sure of, and things they want to know as their study progresses.

On day three, students watch a video about the time period, and then they select one of four journal prompts to complete in their learning logs. The prompts, all dealing with change, are at varying degrees of difficulty, but students are free to write on whichever prompt they choose. They then read their textbook and take notes on their reading using one of three organizers distributed by the teacher. The amount of structure in the organizers varies, and they are given to students based on the teacher's assessment of their skill with reading text materials.

As students read, Mrs. Lupold calls small groups to sit with her on the floor in the front of the room. She works with them on key vocabulary, interpretation of key passages, and direct reading, again based on her awareness of their needs as readers. When students complete reading the chapter, she gives them a quick quiz. At this point, the quiz is not for a grade but to see how to assign students to a key activity she is planning for the next couple of days.

Throughout the year, Mrs. Lupold works with students to identify and transfer key themes of history, guiding them to understand that people in one period have experiences much like those in others. Based on student knowledge and understanding of essential information in the unit to this point—and based on her awareness of their proficiency in reading and thinking about history—she assigns them to one of four groups to identify key themes in the Industrial Revolution. They're also asked to compare the themes to current events.

To begin the activity, Mrs. Lupold reads several portions of Paul Fleischman's *Dateline Troy* (1996). Telling *The Iliad* on the left-hand pages of the book, the author uses clippings from modern newspapers and magazines to demonstrate how closely the events of today parallel those of the ancients. Although the book deals with a period other than the Industrial Revolution, the author models the principle that the struggles of one period are much like those of another.

The four groups in Mrs. Lupold's class are given similar sense-making activities, but they differ for readiness. Mrs. Lupold calls the groups T, R, O, and Y. When she assigned students to the groups, R was the most advanced group and T the next most advanced. Group O was composed of students at or a bit below grade level expectations in reading and knowledge of history. The Y group was having the greatest difficulty with reading, understanding, and interpreting history. For clarity of explanation here, the group designations have been rearranged with T being the most basic group and Y being the most sophisticated.

Group T's instructions imitated what the author of *Dateline Troy* did. For example, students were told, "The author shows us that people used a lottery to see who joined the army 3,000 years ago and in the Viet Nam War. Now, work in pairs and take a second look at the video on the Industrial Revolution. Use it and the textbook to find important things that happened during that time. [The instructions gave some examples of important things.] Check your list of important themes with me before going ahead with rest of the assignment. What you'll do then is watch television news programs to look for current events similar to what was happening in the Industrial Revolution."

Students used a three-column grid provided by the teacher to list their key event in the Industrial Revolution, a current event, and how the two were alike. Ultimately, they were asked to show classmates a news clip and explain how the event in it was like an event in the Industrial

Revolution. They were encouraged to put their grid on the overhead or make their own organizer to use during the explanation. Both partners had to be ready to present.

Students in Group R worked in groups of three. Their instruction sheet first asked them to connect right- and left-hand pages in *Dateline Troy*. (For example, "What is the problem shared by Achilles on page 48 and Darryl Strawberry on page 49?") Next, they were asked to think about key events in the Industrial Revolution and to search sources such as *Time, Scholastic, Newsweek*, and newspapers to find five possible matches. Then they were to select their two best matches, defending to the teacher why the two were "best" before they continued with the task. Ultimately, they created two parallel pages for a book called "Dateline Industrial Revolution." This book contained key events from the Industrial Revolution on the left-hand page and a collage of articles from "matching" news sources on the right. Students were encouraged to use cartoons, computer graphics, headlines, and drawings along with the news articles themselves. All students in the group had to be ready to present, explain, and defend the pages to classmates.

Working in quads, students in Group O were asked to take a look at *Dateline Troy* and create a parallel book excerpt for the Industrial Revolution. They were to select approximately eight events from the Industrial Revolution that demonstrated the revolutionary nature of the time. Then they were to find parallel "revolutions" in this century, create or find collage materials that made the parallels clear, and devise a way to both tell and show the parallel nature of the two revolutions in their own book. Students had to clear their plans for the book segment with the teacher before executing them. They were asked to work for insightful language and visuals. All members of the group had to be prepared to share and interpret their creation.

Group Y students could work in twos, threes, or fours. Their instructions said, "The period we are studying is called the Industrial Revolution, yet there was no army or fighting as in the French Revolution, American Revolution, or Russian Revolution. It's also possible for individuals to have revolutionary experiences. Using *Dateline Troy* as a model, develop a way to think about and show what you would consider to be essential elements in any revolution (such as rapid change, fear, or danger). Your comparison must include the Industrial Revolution, an individual revolution, and a military revolution. It must use important, valid, and defensible themes. It also must be effective in communicating your ideas: accurate, insightful, articulate, visually powerful, and easy to follow."

As the unit drew to a close, the teacher presented a lecture on the Industrial Revolution to highlight information, ideas, and themes she wanted to reinforce. She used the New American Lecture format (Canter & Associates, 1996). She (1) planned the flow of her lecture, (2) developed a graphic organizer that followed the lecture sequence (and that students could use to take notes if they wanted to), and (3) delivered the lecture in four- to six-minute chunks. She followed each chunk with a class discussion and summary of key points.

Next, she asked students in groups T and R to use their tiered activity materials to help her demonstrate how the Industrial Revolution isn't so different from today. Then she had students continue to explore that idea with a "4 X 4" sharing. The sharing groups were made up of one student from each of the four tiered activity groups (although the teacher did not tell students that this was the case). Depending on their group, students were asked to use their dateline materials to illustrate: (1) how the Industrial Revolution relates to our lives, (2) key events in the Industrial Revolution, (3) key themes or elements in the Industrial Revolution, or (4) how the Industrial Revolution was revolutionary. She did not assign a given question to a particular student, but by virtue of the tiered activity, each student was prepared to answer at least one question.

Students then completed a paired review for a quiz on the unit, using a study guide provided by the teacher. It included important vocabulary, events, and themes. Students could select a partner for review. The students then took a quiz. A more engaging assessment of students' grasp of the unit was their completion of a product they began about three-quarters of the way through the unit. They completed it as their study of the next unit began. The product assignment asked students to develop a way to show a revolution in

- a person's life,
- the last 50 years,
- a culture,
- a subject or hobby area, or
- the future.

Students were to show how key concepts and themes (change, scarcity and plenty, interdependence, danger) were reflected in the revolution they explored. They had to draw clear parallels to the Industrial Revolution. Students could express their findings and understandings through a research paper, model, creative writing, drama, music, or other format. They could work alone or in groups of up to four. The teacher provided rubrics to guide product quality, and she encouraged students to modify the rubrics for their products and to present the modified version to her for approval.

Differentiate What: Throughout the unit, the teacher differentiated content (e.g., she used videos as well as text materials), process (e.g., the tiered activity based on *Dateline Troy*), and product (e.g., the product assignment that allowed different applications of key understandings).

Differentiate How: Mrs. Lupold differentiated her teaching in response to readiness, as when she offered novels on two levels for volunteers to read aloud. She also differentiated for readiness when she varied the concreteness/abstractness and structure/openness in the tiered assignment. She differentiated for interest through options for product applications and modes of expression. She differed by learning profile when she gave students choices of working conditions for the product, and she called on varied learning strengths in the tiered activities.

Other Considerations: Mrs. Lupold demonstrated many key principles of differentiation. All students had respectful activities. They were interesting and focused on essential ideas and skills. They were likely to promote both challenge and success for students with varying needs. Students worked in many different groupings: randomly at their tables, with thinking partners of their choice, with another thinking set, alone, with students of like readiness, and with students of mixed readiness. The groupings continually shifted, according to both teacher choice and student choice.

The teacher took great care to support struggling learners: using videos to supplement text materials, breaking a lecture into accessible parts, providing a review guide, building more structure into the tiered assignment. Yet they moved from a concrete look at the events of the Industrial Revolution to a more abstract application. Further, the teacher made certain that advanced learners were challenged. She offered advanced reading materials at several points, provided a very abstract and multifaceted version of the tiered assignment, and allowed opportunities for advanced students to work with peers of similar readiness. She focused on skills of reading, writing, and interpretation with the whole class and with small groups. But the conceptual focus of the unit was meaning-rich for all students. All of her efforts made the Industrial Revolution more meaningful and memorable.

In all the examples of differentiation described in this chapter, teachers were clear about the essential facts, concepts, principles, and skills that framed their subjects. The teachers also continually sought information to help them understand each student's point of entry and progress. Then they attempted to match curriculum and instruction to the learner's readiness, interest, or mode of learning. They wanted to provide students the opportunity to learn coherently, at an appropriate level of challenge, and in an engaging way. Each teacher wanted to link the learner and the learning, a process that's sometimes uncommonly difficult to envision amidst the "one-size-fits-all" classrooms.

Instructional Strategies That Support Differentiation

7

> Only teachers who utilize a variety of instructional
> models will be successful in maximizing the achievement
> of all students. . . . Teachers need to "play to" students'
> strengths and to mitigate students' learning weaknesses.
> This can be done only through the use of instructional
> variety.
> Thomas J. Lasley & Thomas J. Matczynski
> *Strategies for Teaching in a Diverse Society*

There's nothing inherently good or bad about instructional strategies. They are, in essence, the "buckets" teachers can use to deliver content, process, or products. Yet some "buckets" are better suited to achieving one type of goal more than another. The "buckets" can be used artfully or clumsily as part of well-conceived, or poorly conceived, lesson plans and delivery. In addition, virtually all "buckets" can be used in ways that ignore student learning differences, or they can become part of a larger system that appropriately responds to those differences.

For example, it would be grossly inefficient to use the instructional strategy called group investigation to introduce 3rd graders to the concept of fractions. Similarly, it would be ineffective to ask high school students to develop a stance on the ethical issue of genetic engineering using the instructional strategy called concept attainment. Or consider the nest of strategies we call cooperative learning. They have fallen short of expectations not because of a deficiency in the strategies themselves but because teachers apply them shallowly.

Expert teachers generally are comfortable with a wide range of instructional strategies, and they vary them skillfully with the nature of the learning task and learners' needs (Berliner, 1986). When they are correctly used, many instructional strategies invite teachers to respond to students' differences in readiness, interest, or learning profile. Some of the instructional strategies last only a short time during a lesson and require little planning. Others help teachers shape an entire way of life in the classroom and require extensive planning and ongoing reflection. Some of the strategies emphasize organization or arrangement of students for learning. Others focus predominately on the nature of instruction itself.

There are many avenues to creating an instructionally responsive classroom. As you read about instructional strategies in this chapter and the next, observe how teachers use them to create classrooms where students have the opportunity to work at a comfortable pace, at an individually challenging degree of difficulty, in a learning mode that is a good match for their learning profiles, and with applications that are personally intriguing.

As in the last chapter, the instructional strategies are described in actual classroom scenarios and then analyzed with three questions: Differentiate what? Differentiate how? Differentiate why?

Stations

Stations are different spots in the classroom where students work on various tasks simultaneously. They can be used with students of every age and in all subjects. They can be a frequent or occasional part of the learning process. They can be formal or informal. They can be distinguished by signs, symbols, or colors, or the teacher simply can ask groups of students to move to particular parts of the room. (A strategy that is both like and different from stations is centers, which are discussed and illustrated in Chapter 8.)

For the purposes of differentiated instruction, stations allow different students to work with different tasks. They invite flexible grouping because not all students need to go to all stations all the time. Not all students need to spend the same amount of time in each station, either. Further,

even when all students do go to every station, assignments at each station can vary from day to day based on who will rotate there. Stations also lend themselves to a good balance of teacher choice and student choice. On some days, the teacher decides who will go to a particular station, what work they will do when they get there, and the working conditions that must prevail while they are there. On other days, students can make these decisions. On still other days, the teacher may set some of the parameters, but the student can choose the rest.

Grade 4: Math

At the beginning of the year, math assessments show that Ms. Minor's 4th graders are "all over the place" with computation of whole numbers. She has presented the children with a variety of tasks involving computation at varying degrees of sophistication and in varied contexts. This has helped her assess their starting points, and she has discovered that these learners represent quite a range of readiness, from two or three years below grade expectations to an equal distance above grade level.

Some of the 4th graders still have difficulty with basic math facts and algorithms, or rules of computation, in addition or subtraction. These students are really lost with multiplication beyond rote memory of times tables. Other students have a good understanding of the algorithms of number computation for addition, subtraction, and multiplication. They just need extra opportunities to apply their understandings in varied situations. They also are ready to begin a formal exploration of division. Still other students no longer find the three basic operations either interesting or challenging as presented by the grade-level math text. Many of these students have an "instinctive" understanding of division. Some of them have had formal teaching about it, or they have taught themselves how to divide. Another consideration is that students' attention spans vary. Some can lose themselves in math tasks for lengthy periods; others find 10 minutes of concentrated work a strain. Further, Ms. Minor has discovered that length of attention span is not always a function of competency.

To begin the year, Ms. Minor gradually introduces her students to five learning stations, really just areas of the room. Each day, students look at a peg board with nails that represent the five stations in the room. Key tags with student names hang in the various sections of the peg board. In that way, students know where to begin math class.

Station 1 is The Teaching Station. Students in Station 1 have direct instruction with the teacher. They meet with her near the blackboard, and she teaches them and guides their work on a topic in number computation. Often, she leaves students in this group to work at the board or in pairs on the floor. They solve problems or practice skills as she circulates among the other stations. Students at Station 1 record their work at the station by finding their name on a clipboard chart and checking the date and kind of computation on which they worked.

Station 2 is Proof Place. Students in Station 2 use manipulatives or drawn representations to work with number computation and to explain and defend their work. This station helps students understand why numbers and number computations work as they do. They are assigned to the station with a partner, but first they work alone with a computation or series of computations in a folder with their name on it. They time their individual work with a five-minute hourglass. Then they show their partner the tasks they were working on, how they decided what operation to use, and why they think their answers are correct. They may "prove" their work with drawings, diagrams, or manipulatives. Their partner "checks" their understanding by asking them to use a second method for thinking about their answer. Prompts are posted at the station. For example: "Use estimation to show whether your answer is probably right. Show me a diagram or picture that proves your way of thinking about the problem is right. Use the checkers in this cup to show the way you worked the problem is right." Ultimately, students can check a partner's work with the calculator to see if answers agree. Students then complete an "audit" card and attach it to the paper on which the work was done. The audit card says, "Today [student's name] worked on problems using [name of computation] and proved the method by using [diagrams, diagrams, objects]. My partner was [name]. The method we used to check my work was [estimation, objects, diagrams, drawings]. When we checked with the calculator, it said [I was right. I need to think about this some more]." Student date the cards and leave the work and cards in a box at the station. They also "sign out" of the station with a chart. They write the date, check the kind of computation they worked with, and check the method they used to show their thinking.

Station 3 is Practice Plaza. Students in Station 3 practice with the computation on which they need additional experience. They use teacher generated worksheets, computer programs, or a textbook to gain comfort, accuracy, and speed in a particular kind of computation. They check their work using an answer key, calculator, or computer. Finally, they write a self-evaluation about their work, referring, if necessary, to sample language at the station. They leave their signed and dated work in the appropriate box at the station. They also find their name on a chart at the station. It asks for the date, kind of computation they practiced, number of problems attempted, and number correct.

Students in Station 4 work with math applications. Station 4 is The Shop run by a man named Mr. Fuddle, who always seems to need their help. Items in the shop vary from time to time, as do tasks on which students work. But students always work with some facet of running the store or shopping at a store, and they always help Mr. Fuddle, who has somehow gotten himself into another mess.

Sometimes students buy from catalogs. Sometimes they make decisions about what to sell in the store and how much to buy based on a specified budget. Sometimes they count inventory and group items, and sometimes they make change for a series of purchases. Changing objects, varying tasks, and the presence of poor old Mr. Fuddle make going to The Shop fun. The Shop makes math something that is useful in an everyday world. When leaving The Shop, students write notes to Mr. Fuddle, dating them and explaining what problem he has gotten himself into, what they did to solve it, and what he should do next time to avoid the problem. They leave their notes in Mr. Fuddle's mailbox at the station.

Station 5 is Project Place. Here students work alone, in pairs, or in small groups to complete long-term projects that require use of mathematics in a variety of forms. Length of projects vary as do topics. Sometimes projects deal with classroom issues such as designing a center, redesigning the classroom, or conducting and reporting surveys about students. Sometimes they deal with sports, outer space, literature, or writing. Sometimes the teacher thinks of project ideas. Sometimes students do. What all projects have in common is that students use mathematics in a way that connects it to a larger world and in a way that piques student interest. Students keep Project Diaries in which they make two entries whenever they are at Project Place. At the beginning of class, they summarize what they have done so far on their project, and they set goals for the day. At the end of class, they write about how they did with their goals and their next steps. Their Project Diaries stay at the project center in a file box.

Some days, Ms. Minor teaches whole-class math lessons, conducts whole-class reviews, plays whole-class math games, or runs whole-class "contests." On those days, no student names are on the peg board. Occasionally, one or two stations are "closed for the day." Most days, however, students are assigned to one of the five stations to work. All students go to all stations in the course of a week or 10 days. Not all students spend the same amount of time at each station in a given two-week period, and not all students rotate through the stations in the same order. Sometimes students work at a station with students of similar readiness; sometimes they work with students of differing readiness.

Ms. Minor uses students' record-keeping forms, work, and diaries along with periodic formal assessments to assign students to stations. One day, for example, she worked at the Teaching Station with six students to review multiplication of two-digit numbers. Two of those students stayed at the station for a second day, and she added two students who had been working fairly well with two-digit multiplication. They had been sick and absent for several days. Of the four students who left the Teaching Station, two went to the Thinking Place (along with several other pairs of students who were working on a variety of computations). Two others went to Practice Plaza to hone their computation of two-digit numbers. At Project Place, eight students worked on three different long-term projects. In each of the three groups, some members were at other stations that day. Students understand that often group members will work in other places. Project diaries help all members of a group keep up with one another's progress on the joint effort.

Differentiate What: Ms. Minor can differentiate content and process at The Teaching Station, Proof Place, Practice Plaza, and The Shop. All students work with math reasoning, math application, and math practice. But Ms. Minor varies the particular operations, their degree of difficulty, and the degree of difficulty of activities to provide a good fit for students based on her ongoing assessment of their strengths and needs. She differentiates products at Project Place. These vary in complexity, duration, group composition, skills required, and other variables based on her continual assessment of learners' needs.

Differentiate How: Ms. Minor differentiates predominately by student readiness at stations 1–4, with students of similar readiness working on tasks at a similar difficulty level. Station 5 often, but not always, involves students of varying readiness working on projects together. Station 4 (The Shop) addresses interest by varying materials and problems based on the different materials. Station 5 (Project Place) always places a strong emphasis on student interest. It offers a wide range of project options and modes of expression. Learning profile

is addressed by having various ways to think about and demonstrate math reasoning in Proof Place. It also addresses the fact that various students will grasp math through different approaches.

Differentiate Why: Essential understandings and skills about math operations are more accessible to students when presented at their readiness levels. Motivation is high because of the variety of approaches to learning math, varied materials and product options, and the opportunity to work with a variety of students. Further, both teaching and learning are more efficient through the targeted use of stations than would be the case in either whole-class instruction or by having all students remain the same amount of time at each station to complete the same work in each station.

Other Considerations: Ms. Minor uses stations in a way that accentuates the concept of flexible grouping. Even in The Teaching Place, where students need similar direct instruction, students stay for different amounts of time. At Stations 2-4, students of varied readiness levels may work at the same station but on different tasks. Also, since rotation does not progress in a certain order—and because length of assignment to a center varies with student need—students have a sense that "everyone does a bunch of different things" in their math class. They have no sense of specific "math groups." An additional layer of ambiguity about why students work in a given spot at a given time is added as the teacher sometimes assigns students to The Shop based on interest (for example, sending students who like sports to The Shop on a day when materials and tasks revolve around ordering, inventorying, or purchasing athletic materials) and by the pronounced element of student choice in math applications projects at Project Place.

Agendas

An agenda is a personalized list of tasks that a particular student must complete in a specified time. Student agendas throughout a class will have similar and dissimilar elements on them. A teacher usually creates an agenda that will last a student two to three weeks. The teacher develops a new agenda when the previous one is completed.

Generally, students determine the order in which they will complete agenda items. A particular time in the day is set aside as agenda time. In elementary classrooms and block scheduled secondary classrooms, teachers often select the first part of the day or block. In other classes, agendas are used once a week or as anchor activities when students complete other assigned work.

While students work on their agendas, the teacher has great freedom to move among individual students, coaching and monitoring their understanding and progress. The teacher also can take advantage of agenda time to assemble small groups of students who need guided work or direct instruction with a particular concept or skill. (See Figure 7.1 for a sample agenda.)

Grade 5: Various Subjects

As students enter their classroom each morning, they put away their jackets and books, say hello to classmates and their teacher, and go to the box of agendas. After morning announcements, each student completes a daily planning log, which contains the student's goals for the day toward completing agenda tasks. If a student knows he needs teacher assistance, he writes a request for a conference on the board above the agenda box. Students then move to various parts of the room to begin working on their tasks.

Many students work alone with reading, writing, math, or independent investigations. In several places in the room, students cluster in twos or threes, often on carpet squares, to complete collaborative tasks.

After Ms. Clayter, their teacher, circulates to make certain everyone begins work in a focused and orderly manner, she calls three boys to sit with her on the floor near the bookshelves. For the next several minutes, she discusses the HyperCard stack on volcanoes they completed yesterday at the computer. She leads the boys to tell her that their graphics were really impressive. She agrees. She then asks them to review the written goals for the HyperCard project. Among those is the goal that anyone who uses the stack will come away with a clear understanding of what makes a volcano erupt. With her guidance, the boys admit that their stack falls short of this goal. She leaves them to write a plan, which they must present to her, to ensure the HyperCard stack meets all objectives.

Ms. Clayter then moves to a pair of students coauthoring poems. She has paired the two students to work with poetry as part of their agendas because each has something important to teach the other. Jenna is highly imaginative and uses language like a paint brush to make images for her readers, but she lacks persistence when it comes to polishing her work. Han is less fluent with her imagery, in part because English is her second language. She moved to the United States in 2nd grade. On the other hand, Han's love of poetry is electric, and her work ethic is immense. The two girls enjoy working together, and Ms. Clayter knows they can strengthen each other's writing talent. Ms. Clayter asks them to read her their latest piece of writing, tells them several things she finds effective in the poem, and leaves them with

Figure 7.1
Personal Agenda

Personal Agenda* for _____

Starting Date _____

Teacher and student initials at successful completion	Task	Special Instructions
	Complete Hypercard stack showing how a volcano works.	Be sure to show scientific accuracy and computer skill.
	Read your personal choice biography.	Keep a reading log of your progress.
	Practice adding fractions by completing number problems and word problems on pp. 101–106 of the workbook.	Come to the teacher or a friend for help if you get stuck.
	Complete research for an article on why volcanoes are where they are for our science newspaper. Write the article. Have the editor review it with you. Revise as needed.	Watch your punctuation and spelling! Don't let them hurt your great skill at organizing ideas.
	Complete at least 2 spelling cycles.	

*Remember to complete your daily planning log; I'll call you for conferences and instructions.

two challenges to think about as they work for the remainder of agenda time.

Two boys who need additional practice with math are working on a mystery that asks them to select and use appropriate operations to solve a math problem. The math called for is at a relatively basic level, but the mystery format is inviting. The boys keep a record of mysteries they solve to get "promotions points." These earn them certificates and "badges" as math detectives.

As Ms. Clayter creates student agendas, she has three goals: building on strengths, shoring up deficits, and fostering independence. Thus, she places on each student's agenda work focused on each of those areas. In a two- to three-week agenda cycle, all students are likely to work in several subject areas. They'll work with some things they love and some they could do without. All will set and monitor daily and weekly goals. All will work alone and with peers. All will meet with the teacher informally and formally throughout the agenda period, both at the teacher's request and at their own.

Ms. Clayter finds agendas a great way to attend to student differences in readiness, interest, and learning profile. At this one time in the day, she can extend, enrich, and support student growth in all subject areas. Her students love the calm way to ease into the school day, the variety, and the sense of autonomy the agendas provide.

Differentiate What: Ms. Clayter can differentiate virtually anything through agendas. They allow her to differentiate content by varying materials, subjects, topics within subjects, and degree of teacher support. Agendas permit differentiation of process or sense-making by varying the degree of difficulty of tasks as well as ways students make sense of ideas. Agendas also allow for pacing variation. Students can have differing amounts of time to make sense of a particular skill or concept. Agendas facilitate product differentiation by providing time for students to work on long-term products in class where the teacher can monitor and coach their planning, research, quality of thought, and production.

Differentiate How: Once again, agendas allow great flexibility for modifications based on student readiness, interest, and learning profile. Ms. Clayter can form like-readiness or mixed-readiness groups. She can form groups of students whose skills in a

particular area lag, or she can form groups with students who have long since mastered basic expectations. She can point individual students toward materials and tasks they will find appropriately challenging. She can vary working conditions so that auditory, visual, and kinesthetic learning modes are available, or so that students can select spatial, musical, or linguistic avenues of expression, either independently or collaboratively. Agendas also allow her great opportunity to tap into student interest. Agenda time provides a tailor-made chance to have one student work with fractions through music, another with fractions through baseball trading cards, and still another with fractions through stock market reports.

Differentiate Why: Ms. Clayter is a relatively new teacher, but in her classroom she observes a wide range of student interests and needs in all subjects. It is difficult for her to figure out how to modify curriculum and instruction in every subject all day long. Using agendas allows her to concentrate her efforts at differentiation during one time of the day and still be effective in addressing a great array of student needs. She finds she can achieve most of the goals of differentiation through agendas, and she does so in a way that makes her planning manageable.

Complex Instruction

Complex instruction is a rich strategy developed to deal with the sorts of academic ranges that frequently exist in classrooms that are academically, culturally, and linguistically heterogeneous (Cohen, 1994). Its goal is to establish equity of learning opportunity for all students in the context of intellectually challenging materials and through the use of small instructional groups. Like most promising classroom approaches, complex instruction is itself complex, and it requires considerable reflection and planning. The payoff, however, can be immense. It helps establish a classroom in which the contributions of every individual are prized by all students, and high-level instruction is standard fare for all learners.

Complex instruction tasks

• require students to work together in small groups,

• are designed to draw upon the intellectual strengths of each student in the group,

• are open ended,

• are intrinsically interesting to students,

• are uncertain (thus allowing for a variety of solutions and solution routes),

• involve real objects,

• provide materials and instructions in multiple languages (if students in the class represent varied language groups),

• integrate reading and writing in ways that make them an important means to accomplishing a desirable goal,

• draw upon multiple intelligences in a real-world way,

• use multimedia, and

• require many different talents in order to be completed adequately.

An effective complex instruction task does not

• have a single right answer,

• allow for completion more efficiently by one or two students than by the whole group,

• reflect low-level thinking, or

• involve simple memorization of routine learning.

Teachers who skillfully use complex instruction move among groups as they work. They ask students questions about the work, probing their thinking and facilitating understanding. Over time, teachers also delegate increasing authority for learning to students. They then support students in developing the skills needed to manage the authority well.

Two additional—and vital—teacher roles are discovering students' intellectual strengths and "assignment of status." Cohen (1994) reflects that traditional cooperative groups often fail because students know who is "good at school" and who is not. Those who are good are given, or take, responsibility for successful completion of group tasks. Those who are not "good at school" relinquish, or have taken from them, responsibility for successful completion of school tasks. This, says Cohen, stems from the fact that many school tasks are highly dependent on encoding, decoding, computation, and memorization. Those things become synonymous with school success in the minds of students as well as teachers.

Complex instruction seeks tasks that call on a much wider range of intellectual skills, such as generating ideas, asking probing questions, representing ideas symbolically, using rhythm to interpret or express ideas, hypothesizing, or planning. Teachers study students continually and systematically to identify individual strengths. Teachers then design complex instruction tasks that call upon the various student abilities.

In "assignment of status," teachers seek key moments in group work when a student (often one not perceived as "successful" by peers) makes a worthwhile comment or suggestion. The teacher articulates to the group what she heard the student say and why she feels it is a contribution to the work of the whole group. Students begin to see peers in a different light, and they also begin to develop a vocabulary that reflects a wide range of intellectual strengths. Finally, in presenting complex instruction tasks to the class, the teacher leads the students in listing the full range of intellectual tasks required for successful completion of the work. This helps them understand that all students have something of the required strengths, but no one has all of them.

Grade 10: English

In Ms. McCleary's 10th grade English classes, students have been studying how writers' lives and works intertwine. They have read a variety of types of literature this year, including poetry, and they've looked at writing as "mirror and metaphor." That is, they have explored how a piece of writing can become a metaphor for a larger idea, and they have explored how writing holds a mirror up to readers for readers to better understand themselves and their world. Students recently completed a "stepping stones" writing assignment where they diagrammed and wrote about the events in their own lives that were most important in shaping them to be 10th graders.

Today, Ms. McCleary's students will begin work on a complex instruction task. They will work in small groups for the next four or five class periods to complete the task, sharing what they have learned with all other groups during an additional class period. Homework during this time also focuses on the group's tasks. The task will be one key element of student assessment when the marking period ends. Each group received a task card that reads as follows.

We have been working with how writers' lives (and ours) are often metaphors which they (we) create through actions and deeds—including writing. We have also looked how good authors hold up a mirror to readers, allowing readers to reflect upon their own lives and feelings. Robert Frost wrote a poem called "The Road Not Taken." Your task is to analyze the poem as a metaphor for Frost's life and as a mirror of our own. To do that, you should:

1. Find the poem, read it, interpret it, and reach consensus about what's going on in it and what it means.

2. Research Frost's life, making a "stepping stones" diagram similar to the one you created for your own life earlier this month.

3. Develop a soundscape that takes us along Frost's "journey in the woods." Use music; found sounds; sound effects; and appropriate mime, body sculpture, or narration to help your audience understand the feelings that a "journeyer in the woods" would experience as he or she came to straight places, landmarks, or decision points. Be sure you develop a script for your presentation.

4. Create an "overlay" of Frost's life and the poem, using words and images in such a way that they represent the metaphorical relationship between the two.

5. Transfer the key ideas in the poem to the life and experience of a noted person about whom we are all likely to know a little but could learn a little more. Your "transfer" must clearly draw a relationship between the person and the poem and clearly communicate to classmates how literature can help us understand ourselves.

6. Be certain that your final products demonstrate your understanding of metaphor and mirror, the relationship between varied art forms in communicating human meaning, and details of the people and poem with whom/which you are working.

As usual, you should appoint a group

convener, materials monitor, recorder, and
time monitor. Determine the best role for
each person in your group to play in completing your task. Remember, everyone has
strengths to contribute to your group's success. No one has all the strengths needed.
Because your time is limited, you should
develop a written work plan, including a
time line and group conference times. In
the end, be ready to share criteria by which
your group's work should be assessed
(including required elements as well as your
group's sense of what makes a high-quality
presentation). Your group may have up to
20 minutes to make its presentation to one
other group plus a 10-minute question
exchange with students who serve as your
audience and for whom you are an
audience.

Differentiate What: Ms. McCleary can use the
complex instruction sequence to differentiate content by providing books of varying reading levels
and in varied languages along with videos, music,
and other resources. She does this while ensuring
all students focus on the same essential understandings. She differentiates process by providing
multiple segments of a rich task that allow students to make sense of ideas in a range of ways.
Here, product differentiation (the 20-minute presentation) is differentiated in that students will
"specialize" in one facet of the larger project.

Differentiate How: This complex instruction
example provides for readiness differentiation
through use of varied materials, interest differentiation in selection of biographical subjects, and
learning profile differentiation with investigation
and expression through multiple modes of intelligence. It could also be an important learning profile differentiation to provide resource materials

and instructions in multiple languages if the class
contained students for whom English was not their
primary language.

Differentiate Why: Ms. McCleary has differentiated learning and expression options within a
group endeavor rather than individually. She
wants students with differing readiness levels,
interests, and learning profiles to work together in
ways that dignify each student. Thus, she has
opted to use heterogeneous groups and has taken
great pains to provide for individual needs and success within that context.

Orbital Studies

Chris Stevenson (1992, 1997) suggests "orbital
studies" as an ideal way to address both commonalities and differences among middle-level learners. Indeed, the strategy appears easily adapted to
learners at all levels. Orbital studies are independent investigations, generally of three to six weeks.
They "orbit," or revolve, around some facet of the
curriculum. Students select their own topics for
orbitals, and they work with guidance and coaching from the teacher to develop more expertise
both on the topic and on the process of becoming
an independent investigator.

Orbitals work from the premise that all learners
are dignified by developing and sharing knowledge
and skills. This strategy is not unlike the merit
badge system in Scouting except that (1) in orbital
studies students develop their own topics rather
than select from a prescribed list and (2) topics
stem from the curriculum. Stevenson (1992) suggests that initial lists of potential topics be derived
from surveys of student interest, then augmented
by suggestions from parents and mentors (or even
perusing the Yellow Pages!).

Grade 6: Various Subjects

Sixth graders at Hand Middle School like orbital studies because they are interesting and help them be independent. Teachers also like orbitals because they help integrate the curriculum and let teachers see learners at work in their areas of strength and interest.

The 6th grade teachers developed a brochure on orbital studies, explaining to students and parents what an orbital study is, why it is important, and how it works. The brochure is discussed in all classes in the fall when orbitals begin. It's sent home to parents at that time as well. The brochure describes general characteristics of an orbital, such as:

• An orbital study focuses on a topic of student interest related to some facet of the curriculum.

• A student may work on an orbital study for three to six weeks.

• Teachers help students develop a clear question for study, a plan for research, a method of presentation, and criteria for quality.

• Successfully completing an orbital includes keeping a log of time spent on the study, resources used, and ideas and skills gained. It also requires that students provide a written overview of what was learned for teacher review. The student must make a 10- to 20-minute presentation to at least 5 peers, providing a 1-page handout for the audience and using a display or demonstration. The student also must develop and use a way to get peer feedback on the content and presentation.

Throughout the year, each teacher on the team works with individuals and small groups to help them select and focus on a topic, keep a log, find and use resource materials (including print, electronic, and human), plan and use time, measure progress against preestablished criteria for quality,

make effective oral presentations, and distill key ideas for the handout. This is done through mini-workshops with small groups of students who have extra time when a task is completed and with individuals through required conferences on their orbital studies.

All teachers assume responsibility for helping students with planning, research, time management, and presentation, but they also serve as consultants for orbitals in their own areas of interest or expertise. For example, a math teacher may be a science fiction fan or an English teacher may know a great deal about jazz. Teachers and students alike enjoy the fact that teachers have and can share interests and skills in areas they do not teach.

A student invites a teacher to serve as consultant. A teacher generally will accept the invitation, unless he is already involved in a large number of consultations at the time. In that case, the teacher suggests another option from the team of teachers. On this team, teachers make a special effort to help students see how orbital studies can tie what is learned in class to their own talent and interest areas. They also help students see how orbitals can be used to connect various subjects. Students must complete at least one successful orbital study in a year, but they are encouraged to do multiple orbitals. Because the topics are personal and interesting, and because teacher support is abundant, most students keep an orbital study going much of the year.

Right now, Takisha is working on a "talking mural" of unsung U.S. heroes and heroines. That ties her love of art and portraiture to the study of U.S. history. She is researching little-known male and female heroes of varied races and ages who made a difference for the United States. Her mural will reflect that research. Her flair for the dramatic inspired her to write a script that she will record herself to accompany the mural.

Jesse is building a rocket, which calls on him to extend his knowledge of both science and math. It also lets him use his hands in the process, an opportunity he finds too little of in school.

Jake and Ellie are creating a comic book that uses the key elements of literature, but it lets them develop a science fiction plot they'd like to see in all literature.

Lexie is working on her tennis game at a park near her house. This extension of physical education is allowing her to learn from an 8th grader who volunteered to help her improve her serve and strokes. The lessons are videotaped by a couple of her friends and her dad when they have time. Throughout the process, she compares her tapes with those of professionals (provided by her physical education teacher). She ultimately will share what she has learned with peers also interested in tennis.

David is passionate about soccer. He is learning about countries that have been World Cup Soccer Champions, an extension of his studies of geography and culture.

Louis is learning ethnic cooking. This connects with studies of geography and culture. He also feels it's important to learn to cook so he can entertain friends when he gets older and has his own apartment. In the meantime, he tries out what he learns on his family and friends, and he is developing his own cookbook. Other students are working with topics as wide-ranging as superstition, music in Colonial America, science games for young children, and how baseball has changed in the past century.

Much of the work on orbitals is completed at home. However, there are times in each class devoted to working on orbital research and related skills. Students know that when classwork is completed, they may use the extra time to work on their orbital studies. Every other Friday in one class, students present orbitals they have completed. Peers may sign up to attend a presentation in which they are interested, much like adults select sessions at a conference. All attendees provide feedback for the presenters. Students not attending a presentation may work on their own projects, catch up on missed classwork, or use the time to get peer help with some of their work.

Some areas of the room are designated and arranged for orbital presentations. Others are designated and arranged for quiet work by individuals or pairs. If a student in the work area does not have a work plan for the class period, the teacher will provide appropriate work. When there are several orbitals ready for presentation, two classrooms will be designated for presentation only, one for individual or paired work, and one for teacher assistance with work in any subject.

Following their reading and review of orbital study presentations, teachers share the summaries with other teachers on the team. They all make a concerted effort to connect what students are learning about in their orbital studies with what they continue to learn in class. When they miss an opportunity—or sometimes before they seize it—students often remind them of the connections as well.

Differentiate What: Orbital studies allow differentiation of content (because students select their own topics and research materials), process (because students develop their own study plans), and products (because students can select from a wide range of options about how to express their learning). In orbital studies, content, process, and product are differentiated by student choice rather than by teacher choice. Teachers, however, play an active role in coaching students for success in understanding, preparation, and presentation.

Differentiate How: Orbitals focus on differentiation by student interest (because of topic choice and mode of expressing learning) and learning profile (because of the opportunity to determine working conditions and intelligence preference). Again, the teacher assumes a key role in monitoring student choices and progress and coaching for high-quality outcomes.

Differentiate Why: Students are energized by school and the learning process when it belongs to them and when they can shine in what they love to do. Orbitals allow students to exercise choices in what to study and how to share what they learn. Orbitals also provide teachers a systematic way to help young learners become more independent in their learning. As is the case with much, if not all, of differentiation, the goal is for the teacher to meet a student where he is in knowledge, understanding, thought, planning, and presentation, and then to help the learner push forward.

More Instructional Strategies to Support Differentiation

8

> I like this class because there's something different going on all the time. My other classes, it's like peanut butter for lunch every single day. This class, it's like my teacher really knows how to cook. It's like she runs a really good restaurant with a big menu and all.
> Comment from a course evaluation written
> by a 7th grader

There are many strategies that invite teachers to look at needs of small groups and individuals, as opposed to strategies that encourage teachers to teach as though all learners share the same readiness level, interests, and modes of learning. In Chapter 6, we examined stations, agendas, complex instruction, and agendas as tools that facilitate differentiation. In this chapter, we'll look extensively at centers, entry points, tiered activities, learning contracts, and more succinctly at compacting, problem-based learning, group investigation, independent study, choice boards, 4MAT, and portfolios—all useful instructional strategies when a teacher wants to focus on individual or small group needs within a

unit or topic of study explored by all members of the class.

Centers

Teachers have used centers for many years, probably because they are flexible enough to address variable learning needs. Centers differ from stations (discussed in Chapter 6) in that centers are distinct. Stations work in concert with one another. A teacher may create a science center, a writing center, and an art center. But students won't need to move to all of them to achieve proficiency with a topic or set of skills. Consider the math class used to illustrate stations in Chapter 6.

All students rotated among the stations to become competent with various mathematical concepts and skills. Those stations were linked in a way that centers aren't.

Different teachers use centers in different ways; thus, they define them in different ways, too. Two kinds of centers are particularly useful for differentiated instruction: learning centers and interest centers. This section defines and offers guidance about creating these two kinds of centers, but teachers should feel free to modify the suggestions to meet their own and their students' needs.

Defining Centers

A *learning center* is a classroom area that contains a collection of activities or materials designed to teach, reinforce, or extend a particular skill or concept (Kaplan, Kaplan, Madsen, & Gould, 1980). An *interest center* is designed to motivate students' exploration of topics in which they have a particular interest.

In general, centers should

• focus on important learning goals;

• contain materials that promote individual students' growth toward those goals;

• use materials and activities addressing a wide range of reading levels, learning profiles, and student interests;

• include activities that vary from simple to complex, concrete to abstract, structured to open-ended;

• provide clear directions for students;

• offer instructions about what a student should do if he needs help;

• include instructions about what a student should do when he completes a center assignment;

• use a record-keeping system to monitor what students do at the center and the quality level; and

• include a plan for ongoing assessment of student growth in the class in general, which will lead to adjustments in center tasks.

The materials and tasks at learning centers typically are more teacher constructed, though they encourage students to share in designing what and how something will be studied. The materials and tasks focus on mastery or extension of specific understandings or skills. These materials and tasks also are more exploratory than other assignments.

Multi-age Classroom: Dinosaurs

Ms. Hooper teaches in a multi-age classroom with students typically in grades 2 and 3. Like most primary children, these young learners are fascinated by dinosaurs. Ms. Hooper wants to encourage students' natural curiosity about dinosaurs, but she also wants to use the study of dinosaurs to help students understand scientific concepts like patterns, classification, adaptation, and change.

Sometimes the whole class listens to a story or watches a video about dinosaurs, talks about what a dinosaur picture or skeleton can tell them if they think like scientists, or classifies a dinosaur on their classification chart. Ms. Hooper also uses the science center to ensure that students get individual practice with key concepts and skills. For the next couple of weeks, all students will visit the learning center to work like paleontologists to analyze various dinosaur artifacts. They are to explain how dinosaurs adapted to their environments. In this multi-age class, however, students vary widely in sophistication of thought and reading skill. Their previous knowledge about and interest in dinosaurs also varies greatly.

The learning center contains plastic figurines of dinosaurs; pictures of dinosaurs; fossils of bones, teeth, skin, and footprints; replicas of dinosaur skeletons; several books; and some coloring book outlines of dinosaurs. It also includes a variety of art materials and writing tools. Directions are written on cards and recorded on a small tape recorder. Students know they are assigned to the center when they see their name on a chart titled "Paleontologists of the Day."

This week, directions in the center guide students to open a box that contains several artifacts. Next to the box is a clipboard containing a sheet labeled "I Can Think Like a Paleontologist." The student writes her name on the sheet and answers questions by examining and thinking about the artifacts in the box. Students are assigned to this center on several occasions over two weeks. They also may elect to visit the center when it is not in use and when they have student choice time. Students who work with basic tasks at the beginning of the two weeks later may work with tasks that more advanced students completed earlier in the study.

Among today's visiting paleontologists are Gina, almost 9, and Jordan, who is a young 7. Both find reading difficult, and, at this point, they need highly structured learning tasks. Their artifact box contains two models of dinosaur teeth and three plastic models of dinosaurs. They are asked to examine the teeth to predict what the animal eats. They then look at the legs, necks, and hands of the three models and predict what these features suggest. (A portion of their task sheet is shown in Figure 8.1, p. 78.) Finally, they select another dinosaur model from the center and make predictions by examining its features. The tape recorder guides their reading if they choose to use it. Also, to provide more support for their work at the center, Ms. Hooper assigned Gina and Jordan to work together at the center.

On another day, Mishea, an 8-year old, and Carla, who is still 6, are working on a similar task. But their work is designed in response to their advanced reading and classification skills and their large store of knowledge about dinosaurs. Directions are still available on tape. Their artifact box contains fossils of skeletons, bones, and teeth. The teacher has included a number of pictures of dinosaurs with their names. These students, too, must use the artifacts to make predictions about dinosaur adaptation. Figure 8.2 (p. 79) shows a portion of their task sheet. It reflects how their work is more complex and less structured.

Ms. Hooper also uses an interest center on dinosaurs to encourage students to enrich and expand their understanding of topics related to their formal study. Students may sign up to go to the center during student choice time, but they are not required to do so. They also may elect to work alone or with a partner. This center has several tasks proposed by the teacher and a wide range of art, print, and video materials useful for completing the tasks. Students can design their own task by completing an "I Want to Know" planning form and presenting it to the teacher (see Figure 8.3, p. 80).

Among tasks posted at the interest center this week are the following:

• Find out how iguanas are like dinosaurs and draw a comparison picture.

• Read about Chinese dragons and other mythological creatures that may have been inspired by dinosaurs. Share what is learned with the class.

• Make a dinosaur skeleton from clay and chicken bones to show how the dinosaur is adapted to its environment.

Figure 8.1
Dinosaur Worksheets

---

1. The green dinosaur is a Hypsilaphodon.

It has a _____ neck.
  long/short

It is good for _____ .
  eating leaves from tall trees/eating short bushes

It has _____ legs.
long and thin/short and chunky

They are for _____ .
  walking slowly/running fast

To protect itself this dinosaur uses _____ .
  claws/spikes/running/club tail

It uses its long tail _____ .
  to swim/for balance

It uses its long tail _____ .
  to swim/for balance

---

2. The gray dinosaur is Triceratops.

It has a _____ neck, pointy teeth, and a beak.
  long/short

They are good for _____ .
  eating soft leaves from tall trees/
  eating tough low plants

It has _____ legs.
  short and chunky/
  long and thin

They are good for _____ .
  walking slowly/
  running

To protect itself, this dinosaur uses _____ .
  running/claws/
  horn/a club tail

---

3. The brown dinosaur is Euoplocephalus.

It has good legs for _____ .
  running fast/walking

It has a beak which means it probably eats _____ .
  plants/animals

To protect itself it uses _____ .
  running/club tail/
  armor/bony spikes

4. Pick another dinosaur and tell about it. Draw it if you'd like to.

Figure 8.2
I Can Think Like a Paleontologist

Dinosaur	Legs	Tail	Teeth	Other Trait
Hypsilophodon 	Kind For	Kind For	Kind For	Kind For
Triceratops 	Kind For	Kind For	Kind For	Kind For
Euoplocephalus 	Kind For	Kind For	Kind For	Kind For
Tyrannosaurus 	Kind For	Kind For	Kind For	Kind For
Stegosaurus 	Kind For	Kind For	Kind For	Kind For
Your Choice (Give Name)	Kind For	Kind For	Kind For	Kind For

Figure 8.3
I Want to Know

My question or topic is _____

_____

_____

To find out about it, I will _____

I will read

I will look at and listen to

I will draw

I will write

I will need

I will finish by _____ .   I will share what I learned by

• Find out three things scientists think might have caused the extinction of dinosaurs. Make posters to tell the class about the three ideas.

• Find out about today's reptiles that are relatives of dinosaurs. Make drawings or models that compare them to dinosaurs.

• Write a job description for a paleontologist that explains what the person does and what kind of training is needed.

Differentiate What: In the learning center, Ms. Hooper differentiates materials (a part of content) while ensuring that all students practice essential concepts and skills. She also differentiates process as she develops activities at varied levels of complexity. At the interest center, Ms. Hooper differentiates content by giving students choices about what to study. She differentiates process by varying the ways students learn. She differentiates product by offering varied options for students to demonstrate their learning.

Differentiate How: Using the learning center allows Ms. Hooper to differentiate instruction by student readiness level. (She varies the complexity of resources and task to match students' starting points.) Interest centers focus on a variety of student interests, and they include the option for students to propose their own studies. In both the learning center and the interest center, the teacher can attend to learning profile differences by having students work alone or with peers; presenting visual and auditory directions; and providing resources that contribute to kinesthetic, visual, spatial, and linguistic strengths.

Differentiate Why: In a multi-age primary classroom, differences in readiness, background knowledge, interest, and learning profile are evident, although not necessarily by age or grade. By having students work together, individually, or in small groups, the teacher creates community learning experiences and attends to individual needs. By sometimes having students work on the same learning center tasks at different chronological points, the teacher's planning is made easier. She also effectively escalates student growth. Further, there is a balance between student choice and teacher choice in use of centers. The teacher makes key assignments to the learning center, but students may elect to return to the learning center. They initiate their own involvement with the interest center.

Entry Points

Howard Gardner (e.g., 1993) has contributed greatly to the awareness that students vary in intelligence preferences or strengths. Through his continuing investigation of multiple intelligences, he has helped educators understand that a child who is strong spatially may take in information, solve problems, and express learning differently than a child whose strength is verbal-linguistic. While Gardner is clear that intelligences are interrelated, he also is convinced that there are important differences among them. Teachers can facilitate the learning process by attending to these differences when planning and carrying out instruction.

Gardner (1991, 1993) has described "Entry Points" as a strategy for addressing varied intelligence profiles. He proposes student exploration of a given topic thorough as many as five avenues or Entry Points:

• Narrational Entry Point: Presenting a story or narrative about the topic or concept in question.

• Logical-Quantitative Entry Point: Using numbers or deductive/scientific approaches to the topic or question.

- Foundational Entry Point: Examining the philosophy and vocabulary that undergird the topic or concept.
- Aesthetic Entry Point: Focusing on the sensory features of the topic or concept.
- Experiential Entry Point: Using a hands-on approach where the student deals directly with materials that represent the topic or concept. These materials also make links to the student's personal experience.

Grade 7: The Middle Ages

Ms. Boutchard is about to begin an exploration of the Middle Ages in Europe with her 7th grade history students. She has decided to introduce them to the culture and thought of the time by having them investigate cathedrals. A medieval cathedral is an exemplar—almost a metaphor—for much of the time period. She believes students will have a far richer platform for understanding the period and its people if they understand the technology used in building cathedrals, what it meant to be an architect during that time, raw materials that were available, the occupational system that supported the crafting and construction of these amazing structures, and the belief system that made them so important.

Students in Ms. Boutchard's class begin their focus on the Middle Ages with a whole-class discussion of what students think of when they hear that term. This gives students a chance to link previous understandings with the learning to come. It gives their teacher a chance to informally get a sense of students' level and depth of knowledge about the time period.

She then gives each student a choice of "signing on" to any one of the five "Entry Points"

investigations. Students may elect to work alone or in a group of up to four. The teacher also has developed an assignment sheet for each investigation, including specific criteria for success. Following are brief capsules of the longer explanations Ms. Boutchard gave to students.

- **Cathedrals Tell Stories (*Narrational Entry*):** Use stories provided by the teacher or find others in which a cathedral is an important feature (almost a character) in the plot. Develop a glossary of terms about a cathedral from information in the story (not from a dictionary or encyclopedia). Show through drawings and supporting written explanations how the author(s) used the cathedral to help shape the story. Write or orally tell a tale or adventure of your own in which you use the cathedral as a "central figure" in the story.
- **Builders of a Legacy (*Logical-Quantitative Entry*):** Using resource materials provided by the teacher and other materials you may find, develop a model that shows the key features of a cathedral and the kind of engineering knowledge and skills the builders used to construct them. It's important to think about knowledge and skill available to engineers now in comparison to those of the Middle Ages.
- **It All Means Something (*Foundational Entry*):** Cathedrals are full of symbols. Find a way to show and explain how the floor plan, art, decorations, and other elements help us understand the beliefs of the people who built and worshiped in cathedrals in the Middle Ages. The teacher has provided resource materials for a starting point. You'll probably want to find others as well.
- **Beauty in the Eye of the Beholder (*Aesthetic Entry*):** Using resource materials provided by the teacher and others you may find, develop a way to show how the architecture, art, and music

of the cathedral tells us what people of the Middle Ages thought was beautiful, and why. You may find it useful to compare their beliefs about beauty with some of our own time period.

- **Your "Cathedral" (*Experiential Entry*):** Most of us have "places" that make us pause, think, wonder, or feel at peace. Some of these are places of worship built by architects and engineers. Others are simple places that take on special meaning to our lives. Using the list of elements of a cathedral and articles on cathedrals provided by the teacher, find a way to show either one or more of your "cathedrals," or someone else's that you know about. Help the class see how the "cathedrals" you select are like cathedrals in the Middle Ages in important ways.

Differentiate What: Ms. Boutchard has differentiated content by providing a range of research materials for each group. These materials support varied reading sophistication. She has differentiated process by providing varied ways to think about cathedrals. The products students create will show what they have learned in varied forms. What stays the same for all students is the need to think about what a cathedral is and what it reveals about the people and the time it represents.

Differentiate How: Interest and learning profile are the predominate emphases of differentiation. Students can select the investigation that seems most intriguing to them, specialize in an area of intelligence preference, select working conditions, and make many choices about how to express what they learn. The teacher supports some readiness differentiation by initially providing resource materials at a range of reading levels.

Differentiate Why: By introducing a topic of study through various intelligence and interest-based lenses, the teacher taps into student strengths and prior experiences. Thus, she enhances motivation, success, and understanding of the same subject among students whose learning profiles and interests differ in important ways. Despite the different modes of learning, however, each student comes away from the "Entry Points" investigations with a common understanding of the time period and people of the Middle Ages. This will help them connect and make sense of facts, concepts, and principles in the rest of the unit.

Tiered Activities

Tiered activities are very important when a teacher wants to ensure that students with different learning needs work with the same essential ideas and use the same key skills. For example, a student who struggles with reading or has a difficult time with abstract thinking nonetheless needs to make sense of the pivotal concepts and principles in a given chapter or story. Simultaneously, a student who is advanced well beyond grade expectations in that same subject needs to find genuine challenge in working with the same concepts and principles. A "one-size-fits-all" activity is unlikely to help a struggling or grade-level learner come to own important ideas. And it won't extend the understanding of a student with great knowledge and skill in the same area.

Teachers use tiered activities so all students focus on essential understandings and skills but at different levels of complexity, abstractness, and open-endedness. By keeping the focus of the activity the same, but providing routes of access at varying degrees of difficulty, the teacher maximizes the likelihood that (1) each student comes away with pivotal skills and understandings and (2) each student is appropriately challenged.

There is no recipe for developing a tiered activity, but the following guidelines are useful for planning (see Figure 8.4).

• Select the concept(s), generalization(s), and skill(s) that will be the focus of the activity for all learners. These are the elements the teacher knows are essential to helping students build a framework of understanding of the topic.

• Think about the students for whom you are planning the activity. Use assessments (journal entries, class discussions, quizzes) related to the upcoming lesson to help you think about the range of readiness for the topic. Add to that your awareness of students' talents, learning profiles, and interests. This need not be an involved process. Just take a few minutes to consider the individuals the activity should reach.

• Create one activity, or draw on one you've successfully used in the past. It should be interesting, require high-level thought, and clearly focus on elements that will cause students to use a key skill(s) to understand a key idea(s).

• Think about, or actually draw, a ladder. The top rung represents students with very high skill and high complexity of understanding. The bottom rung represents students with low skill and low complexity of understanding. Thinking about the students who will use the lesson you developed, decide where the lesson should be placed on the ladder. In other words, will the lesson really stump your most advanced students? Is it likely to challenge grade-level students? Or will it challenge less advanced students? Once you visualize this kind of ladder, you can see who needs another version of the lesson.

• "Clone" the activity along the ladder to provide different versions at different degrees of difficulty. There is no magic number of versions.

Sometimes two will do. Sometimes three, four, or even five may work better to reach a wide range of learners. Cloning occurs when you vary materials students will use (from very basic to challenging for even the most advanced students). Cloning occurs when you allow students to express learning in ways that range from very familiar to unfamiliar. It occurs when you develop a range of applications, from those that closely relate to students' experiences to those that are far removed. (See the Appendix for a discussion of "The Equalizer," which can help teachers with this "cloning" process.)

• Match a version of the task to each student based on student need and task requirements. The goal is to match the task's degree of difficulty and its pacing to student readiness. (Though you want to stretch the student slightly beyond his comfort zone.)

Grade 8: Ozone

Mrs. Lightner's 8th grade students are studying the atmosphere. They have had class discussions, read text materials, viewed videos, and completed a whole-class activity. It is essential that all students understand what ozone is and why it is important in the atmosphere. Mrs. Lightner wants each student to create a foundation for constructing additional knowledge and understanding.

Her assessment of current student understanding, and her ongoing awareness of student reading and thinking profiles, lead Mrs. Lightner to conclude that a tiered activity would enable all her students to experience challenge and develop deeper understanding of the importance of ozone. Based on her sense of student needs, she "cloned" one activity on ozone, which she had previously used. Then she matched the various versions to

Figure 8.4
Developing a Tiered Activity

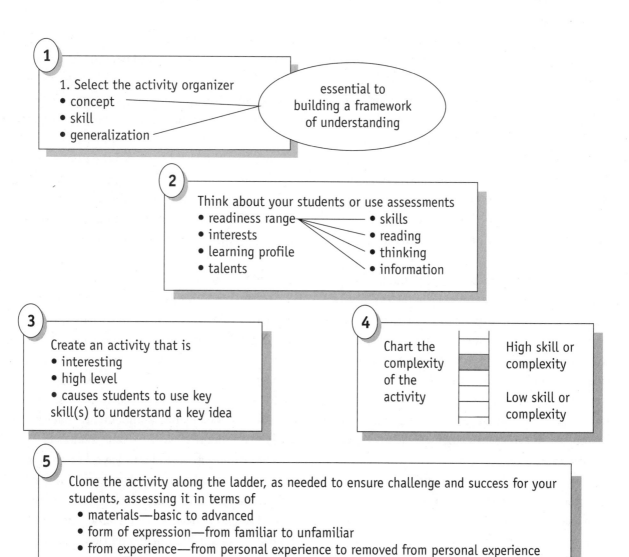

1 1. Select the activity organizer
- concept
- skill
- generalization

essential to building a framework of understanding

2 Think about your students or use assessments
- readiness range
- interests
- learning profile
- talents

- skills
- reading
- thinking
- information

3 Create an activity that is
- interesting
- high level
- causes students to use key skill(s) to understand a key idea

4 Chart the complexity of the activity

High skill or complexity

Low skill or complexity

5 Clone the activity along the ladder, as needed to ensure challenge and success for your students, assessing it in terms of
- materials—basic to advanced
- form of expression—from familiar to unfamiliar
- from experience—from personal experience to removed from personal experience
- the equalizer

6 Match a version of the task to a student based on student profile and task requirements.

individual students. Here is a capsule of elements in the tiered activity, which had four versions.

• All students had some individual and some group tasks to complete.

• All students received a packet of printed material on what ozone is, how it works, and why it is important. The reading level of the various packets varied, however, from below grade level to college-level readability.

• All students were required to take notes on essential information in the packets. Some students were given a note-taking matrix to guide their work. Others simply were asked to take careful notes on a list of key ideas. The teacher monitored all student notes for clarity and thoroughness.

• All students were asked to use the Internet to expand their understanding of the importance of ozone. Students were directed to a variety of sites, which ranged in complexity. Some provided basic information; some were used by practicing professionals. In addition, all students were encouraged to find other useful Internet sites. All students had to appropriately cite the Internet sources, and they had to add to their notes what they learned from the Internet resources.

• To demonstrate understanding of what ozone is and why it is important, each student worked with one or two others to complete the same version of an activity. They drew upon the Internet resources and their notes to apply what they had learned.

For example, the group having the most difficulty with comprehending this topic was asked to write a public service television or radio announcement for citizens of New Zealand, where ozone depletion is a real health hazard. These students used jingles, slogans, and art to convey to their viewing and listening audience why ozone matters, how its depletion puts them at risk, and what they should do to take precautions.

A group with a bit more skill in reading and comprehending this type of scientific material was asked to conduct a survey of peer awareness and understanding about the ozone. They used a professionally constructed survey to serve as a model for designing, conducting, analyzing, and reporting their own survey. The teacher limited the number of questions they could ask and the number of students they could poll to (1) make the task manageable and (2) focus it on essential issues. They had a choice of ways to report their findings: newscast with appropriate graphics, story boards, or a series of charts. Whatever format they selected had to convey both findings and implications.

Students in a third group, who were generally at or slightly above grade level in this area, were asked to write a position paper on the degree to which human activity may or may not negatively impact the ozone cycle. The position paper was to be for a newsletter or news magazine with an audience of upper elementary students. All viewpoints had to be supported with credible evidence.

A fourth group of students was asked to debate the issue of whether there is an ozone problem to which humans contribute. Each debater represented someone from a specific environmental or political group, which held a particular set of beliefs. All debaters had to reflect the viewpoint of their group and simultaneously refute or respond to opposing perspectives.

Differentiate What: In this illustration, Mrs. Lightner has differentiated content by presenting students with reference materials at differing readability levels and suggesting varying Internet sites. What she has not differentiated is the essential understanding of what ozone is and why it is important to living things. She has differentiated process by varying the amount of support given for note taking, and the level of complexity, abstractness, and multifacetedness of the demonstrations of understanding. What she does not differentiate in process is the need for all students to use print and Internet resources, distill information, develop and apply understandings, and share with peers what they have learned.

Differentiate How: A tiered lesson focuses primarily on readiness differentiation. However, the teacher also can address interest or learning profile differentiation by encouraging students to propose alternate forms of expressing what they learn, varying group size, allowing students to work alone, providing recordings of resource materials, or varying time allowed for the tasks.

Differentiate Why: Mrs. Lightner has two key goals in developing this tiered activity. First, she wants all students to have a real understanding of what ozone is and how its presence or absence affects their world. Second, she wants them all to work hard in order to succeed with achieving and demonstrating those understandings. The carefully focused tiered activity maximizes the chance the two goals will be realized for each student in the class. A side benefit to the tiered activity is that while students are busy with their research and application, she is free to work with small groups on reading, comprehension, scientific writing, use of the Internet, or note taking.

Learning Contracts

There are many approaches to using learning contracts (e.g., Berte, 1975; Knowles, 1986; Tomlinson, 1997; Winebrenner, 1992), but each approach includes an opportunity for students to work somewhat independently on material that is largely teacher-directed. In essence, a learning contract is a negotiated agreement between teacher and student that gives students some freedom in acquiring skills and understandings that a teacher deems important at a given time. Many learning contracts also provide opportunities for student choice regarding some of what is to be learned, working conditions, and how information will be applied or expressed. A contract

• Assumes it is the teacher's responsibility to specify important learnings and make sure students acquire them.

• Assumes students can take on some of the responsibility for learning themselves.

• Delineates skills that need to be practiced and mastered.

• Ensures students will apply or use those skills in context.

• Specifies working conditions to which students must adhere during the contract time (student behavior, time constraints, homework and classwork involvement in the contract).

• Sets positive consequences (continued freedom, grades) when students adhere to working conditions. It also sets negative consequences (teacher makes work assignments and sets working parameters) if students do not adhere to working conditions.

• Establishes criteria for successful completion and quality of work.

• Includes signatures of agreement to terms of the contract by both teacher and student.

Grade 4: Poetry

Ms. Howe and her 4th graders are studying poetry. During the course of the three-week language arts unit, students will work with concepts such as rhyme, imagery, and sensory description. They will work with the following key principles:

- Poetry helps readers understand and appreciate their world.
- Poetry uses precise, powerful language.
- Poetry helps us see and think better.

Students will practice skills such as use of rhyming words, elaboration of images and ideas, making metaphors, and punctuation.

Some of the poetry unit uses whole-class instruction to introduce terms (such as metaphors, similes, rhyme) and to acquaint students with numerous poetic forms (such as clerihews, cinquains, haiku, acrostic poems). They also work together simply to enjoy exploring poets' works. Sometimes all students work with the same activity, such as an exercise on creating similes that describe people and things in the classroom. At other times they work on a similar activity, such as a paired practice in which students add punctuation to poems. But the teacher varies the poems she assigns based on complexity of the punctuation task and student skill with punctuation.

A major part of the poetry unit is completed through a learning contract. Each student has a grid with 12 squares. Each square contains an abbreviated explanation of a task that must be completed during the course of the poetry unit. Three times a week during the unit, students have a contract period when they work with their contract grid. When an item on the grid is completed and reviewed by a peer for accuracy and quality, they file it in a stack tray labeled with a heading that matches the corresponding box on the contract grid.

There are two different contract grids in the class. Both look a great deal alike. Both have similar (but not always identical) headings. Both also have three empty cells in which students can insert their own tasks or repeat one they especially liked.

The teacher grades students on the contract portion of the unit in three ways. First, each student gets a grade based on how well they worked (had a goal, worked steadily toward it, adhered to working conditions). Second, she spot checks one or two assignments from each student's grid to check for completion, accuracy, and quality. Third, each student selects two pieces from the contract to become part of a class book on poetry. Those two pieces are assessed by the student, a peer, and the teacher according to a quality checklist posted in the class for each type of poem.

Figures 8.5 and 8.6 are the two contract grids used as a part of this unit. Note that one contract has a circle in each cell and the other has a square. Students check off the circles and squares as they complete their work, but those icons have an additional use. The contract with the circles (Figure 8.5) is completed by students for whom writing and interpreting poetry is new or more difficult. The contract with the squares (Figure 8.6, p. 90) is completed by students who are ready for advanced work with poetry. The two symbols makes it easier for the teacher to note which contract is which at a glance. Students seem unaware of the use of different symbols.

The two versions of the contract give each student experience practicing discrete skills (such as working with figures of speech and interpreting a poem). They also offer the chance to try to incorporate those skills in creating poetry. Variations in the cells are one way the teacher addresses readiness differences. For example, writing a cinquain is more straightforward than writing a diamonte, and

Figure 8.5
Poetry Contract

Name _____

Create a Rhyming Wheel ◯ Use your spelling lists as a way to get started.	**Use Your Rhyming Wheel** ◯ Write a poem that sounds like Shel Silverstein might have written it.	**Write an Acrostic Poem** ◯ Be sure it includes alliteration.
Write ◯ A cinquain (check with another cinquain writer to make sure you got the pattern right).	**Computer Art** ◯ Use clip art to illustrate a simile, metaphor, or analogy on our class list, or ones you create.	**Write About You** ◯ Use good descriptive words in a poem that helps us know and understand something important about you.
Interpret ◯ "How to Eat a Poem"	**Research a Famous Person** ◯ Take notes. Write a clerihew that uses what you learned. (It can have more than one stanza.)	**Illustrate a Poem** ◯ Find a poem we've read that you like, or one on your own. Illustrate it. Write about why you illustrated it as you did.
Student Choice #1 ◯ _____ _____ _____	**Student Choice** #2 ◯ _____ _____ _____	**Student Choice** #3 ◯ _____ _____ _____

Figure 8.6
Poetry Contract

Name _____

Create a Rhyming Wheel ☐ Use your spelling lists and the dictionary as a way to get started.	**Use Your Rhyming Wheel** ☐ Write a poem about something that makes you laugh or smile.	**Write an Acrostic Poem** ☐ Be sure it includes alliteration and onomatopoeia.
Write ☐ A diamonte (Check with another diamonte writer to make sure you got the pattern.)	**Computer Art** ☐ Use clip art to illustrate a simile, a metaphor, and an analogy you create.	**Write About You** ☐ Use good description, figurative language, and images to write a poem that helps us understand something important about you.
Interpret ☐ "Unfolding Bud."	**Research a Famous Person** ☐ Take notes. Write a bio-poem that uses what you learned.	**Illustrate a Poem** ☐ Find a poem you like that we have not read in class. Illustrate the poem in a way that helps the reader understand its meaning. Write about why you illustrated it as you did.
Student Choice #1 ☐ _____ _____ _____	**Student Choice** #2 ☐ _____ _____ _____	**Student Choice** #3 ☐ _____ _____ _____

interpreting "How to Eat a Poem" is more concrete than interpreting "Unfolding Bud," even though both are poems about poetry.

Another way the teacher addresses readiness differences is through directions. For example, directions that accompany the contract with the circles ask students to read "How to Eat a Poem," illustrate it, summarize what it says, and write about what it means or what others can learn from it. Directions accompanying the contract with the squares ask students to read "Unfolding Bud," paraphrase it, and explain what it helps the reader understand about a poet and his or her poetry. Students also are asked to write a similar poem about poetry, or some other subject, that uses a metaphor as that author does.

Ms. Howe's students love the sense of freedom and responsibility they have in planning a time line to complete their work, making choices about what to do on which day, and deciding what goes in the empty grid cells. Ms. Howe enjoys the freedom the contract time gives her. She can have individual conferences with students on poetry or on other facets of their work that need her attention.

Differentiate What: Contracts allow the teacher to differentiate content (kinds of poems to be written and interpreted, resource materials) and process (varying directions). Still, all students work with the same essential concepts, understandings, and skills.

Differentiate How: As used by Ms. Howe, contracts allow differentiation by readiness (different poems, directions, materials), interest (student choice cells), and learning profile (students making decisions about when and how to work on tasks).

Differentiate Why: Use of contracts allows students to engage with poetry at a level of sophistication that enhances the likelihood that each student can feel challenged and successful. Further, the balance of whole-class instruction and contract work offers a good mix of teacher direction and student centeredness.

Other Strategies That Invite Differentiation

A myriad of instructional and management strategies invite teachers to break classes into smaller learning units. Subdividing the class enables the teacher to think about variation in student need and to create groups that attend to student learning differences. All of this can be accomplished while still ensuring that all students work with engaging, high-level tasks focused squarely on essential learning.

The following resource list suggests just a few more of the many strategies that make it natural to differentiate instruction. (For additional information on these strategies, see the resource list at the end of this chapter.) Add your own favorite strategies to the list. This list should be endless; it should grow as we grow more expert at creating academically responsive classrooms.

Compacting

Compacting encourages teachers to assess students before beginning a unit of study or development of a skill. Students who do well on the preassessment (getting as much as three-quarters correct) should not have to continue work on what they already know. With three-stage compacting, teachers document (1) what the student already knows (and evidence for that conclusion), (2) what the preassessment indicates the student does not know about the topic or skill (and plans for how the student will learn those things), and (3) a plan for meaningful and challenging use of time the student will "buy" because she already knows much of the topic or skill. Compacting begins with a focus on student readiness and ends with an emphasis on student interest.

Problem-Based Learning

This approach to learning places students in the active role of solving problems in much the same way adult professionals perform their jobs. The teacher presents students with an unclear, complex problem. Then students must seek additional information, define the problem, locate and appropriately use valid resources, make decisions about solutions, pose a solution, communicate that solution to others, and assess the solution's effectiveness. The strategy calls upon varied learning strengths, allows use of a range of resources, and provides a good opportunity for balancing student choice with teacher coaching. It also offers an opportunity to address student readiness, interest, and learning profile.

Group Investigation

Focusing on student interest, this strategy carefully guides students through investigation of a topic related to something else being studied in class. The teacher guides students through selection of topics and breaks the class into groups by learner interest. Then she helps them with planning the investigation, carrying out the investigation, presenting findings, and evaluating outcomes both individually and as a group. This strategy also provides the opportunity to address student readiness through varying complexity of research materials.

Independent Study

Most students need help to learn how to become independent learners. Throughout all grades, subjects, and readiness levels, teachers should systematically aid students in developing curiosity, pursuing topics that interest them, identifying intriguing questions, developing plans to find out more about those questions, managing time, setting goals and criteria for work, assessing progress according to those goals and criteria, presenting new understandings to audiences who can appreciate them—and beginning the cycle again.

Independent study is a tailor-made opportunity to help students develop talent and interest areas, as long as teachers understand that the independent study needs to meet students at their current readiness for independence and move them toward greater independence a little at a time. Independent study allows emphasis on student readiness, interest, and learning profile.

Choice Boards

With choice boards, changing assignments are placed in permanent pockets. By asking a student to make a work selection from a particular row, the teacher targets work toward student need and at the same time allows student choice. Choice boards are well-suited to dealing with readiness and interest differences among students. For young nonreaders, the cards can be coded with icons or colors. For older students, the cards may use words to designate a task or area of the room. In either case, full instructions for the task are given at the place the student works, not on the choice board itself. Put another way, the choice board simply allows the teacher to "direct traffic."

4MAT

This complex but useful approach to teaching focuses on teacher response to student learning profile. Based on several personality and learning inventories, 4MAT hypothesizes that students have one of four learning preferences. Teachers who use 4MAT plan instruction for each of the four preferences during the course of several days on a give topic. Thus, some lessons focus on mastery, some on understanding, some on personal involvement, and some on synthesis. All students take part in all approaches based on the belief that, in this way, each learner has a chance to approach the topic through preferred modes and also to strengthen "weaker" areas.

Portfolios

These collections of student work are excellent for helping children set appropriate learning goals and evaluate their growth. They also are a powerful means of helping teachers and parents reflect on student growth over time. They can be integral to every part of instruction at every age. They also allow focus on readiness, interest, and learning profile. Portfolios are motivating because of a heavy emphasis on student choice. They also provide an ongoing channel of assessment, which helps teachers see students as individuals. All of this is invaluable in a differentiated classroom.

For More Information

1. For more information on compacting, see
Reis, S., & Renzulli, J. (1992). Using curriculum compacting to challenge the above average. *Educational Leadership 50*(2), 51-57.

Starko, A. (1986) *It's about time: Inservice strategies for curriculum compacting.* Mansfield Center, CT: Creative Learning Press.

2. For more information on problem-based learning see
Delisle, R. (1997). *How to use problem-based learning in the classroom.* Alexandria, VA: Association for Supervision and Curriculum Development.
Torp, L., & Sage, S. (1998). *Problems as possibilities: Problem-based learning for K–2 education.* Alexandria, VA: Association for Supervision and Curriculum Development.
Johnson, T. (1997). *Problem-based learning.* [Videotape and facilitator's guide.] Alexandria, VA: Association for Supervision and Curriculum Development.
Stepien, W. J., & Gallagher, S. (developers) (1997). *Problem-based learning across the curriculum.* [An ASCD Professional Inquiry Kit]. Alexandria, VA: Association for Supervision and Curriculum Development.

3. For more information on group investigation see
Sharan, S. (Ed.). (1994). *Handbook of cooperative learning methods.* Westport, CT: Greenwood Press.
Sharan, Y., & Sharan, S. (1992). *Expanding cooperative learning through group investigation.* New York: Teachers College Press.

4. For more information on independent study see
Tomlinson, C. (1993). Independent study: A flexible tool for encouraging academic and personal growth. *Middle School Journal 25*(1), 55-59.
Treffinger, D. (1978). Guidelines for encouraging independence and self-direction among gifted students. *Journal of Creative Behavior, 12*(1), 14-20.

5. For more information on choice boards see

Madea, B. (1994). *The multi-age classroom: An inside look at one community of learners.* Cypress, CA: Creative Teaching Press.

6. For more information on 4MAT see

McCarthy, B. (1996). *About learning.* Barrington, IL: Excel.

7. For more information on portfolios see

Clemons, J., Laase, L., Cooper, D., Areglado, N., & Dill, M. (1993). *Portfolios in the classroom: A teacher's sourcebook.* New York: Scholastic.

Danielson, C., & Abrutyn, L. (1997). *An introduction to using portfolios in the classroom.* Alexandria, VA: ASCD.

Kingore, B. (1993). *Portfolios.* Des Moines, IA: Leadership Publishers.

How Do Teachers Make It All Work?

9

> Students at work create various kinds of noise. They
> talk and measure and puzzle out and make the audible
> messes that an assistant principal is supposed to abhor.
> Their activity also exposes the inconvenient truth that
> some kids do the work faster than others. The neat
> march over material that is possible when only the
> teacher sets the pace of the journey is no longer possible.
>
> Theodore Sizer
> *Horace's School*

To this point, we largely have focused on issues related to differentiating the curriculum. The curriculum is essential; it is the heartbeat of teaching. But classroom management is important, too. It is the central nervous system of the classroom. Without the heart, there is no life, but without the nervous system, there is no function. This chapter focuses on classroom management that supports differentiated instruction.

Images of School

We all have our own images of "how to do school." Parents base their images on the 13 or more years they spent in school. As teachers, we create different images of school: from our own early schooling through professional training to our first years teaching in the classroom. Students create their images of school day after day in their pilgrimages to become "educated."

Images of school also are fueled by cartoons, movies, television, and books. As a rule, these images are dominated by rows of desks and a teacher working in front of the group. Students wait passively—slouched or wiggling—for the teacher to do whatever she had in mind for the day. Few of these images prepare us even to envision, let alone craft, classrooms that are differentiated in response to the array of children's learning needs.

Alas, there is no fail-safe way to master the alternate approaches to teaching and learning that common sense (and tomes of research) tells us would be more effective. This chapter cannot provide all the answers, either. It can, however, offer broad guidelines for those who seek more promising ways of thinking about, planning for, and being leaders in differentiated classrooms.

Getting Started

If the notion of a student-centered, differentiated classroom is new to you, here are a few suggestions to help you steer your thinking and planning in that direction.

Examine Your Philosophy About Individual Needs

A young teacher working hard to implement a differentiated classroom recently reflected, "Differentiated instruction isn't a strategy. It's a way of thinking about all you do when you teach and all that the kids do when they learn." Not only is she correct, but her insight offers important guidance.

Instead of first focusing on what to do in the classroom, it's wisest to focus on how to think about teaching and learning.

• Which makes better sense to you: that you do most of the work in the classroom, or that students are the primary workers and thinkers? Why?

• Does it seem more likely to you that everyone should always need the same book, math problem, or art lesson? Or are students likely to show up at different points of readiness for reading and math and drawing? Why?

• Do students all seem to learn in the same way or at the same pace? Or do some process information differently and at a different pace than others? How do you know?

• Do you learn more about students by talking *to* them or talking *with* them? Why?

• Do students become independent learners in classrooms where they are always told what to do? Or do they become independent when teachers systematically give them more responsibility for learning and teach them how to use the independence wisely? Why?

• Do learners care if they have choices about what and how to learn? Do they care a lot or a little? Why?

• Are we most motivated to grow when we try to reach our own ceilings or when the ceilings are someone else's? Why do you say so?

• In general, are you more effective and efficient at teaching with small groups of students and individuals, or are you more effective with the whole class? Why do you say so?

• Is learning richer and more permanent when it's rote or meaning based? How do you know?

Add your own questions about teaching to this list. There should be an unlimited supply of them. In the end, your evolving beliefs about your classroom will guide your choices as you plan for and reflect on instruction. Knowing what you believe also will help you feel more comfortable and confident in answering students', colleagues', administrators', and parents' questions about why you teach as you do.

Start Small

Like students, teachers are ready for differing degrees of challenge. Many teachers successfully start differentiating instruction with small, well-organized changes. Here are some suggestions. Use the ones that make sense for your starting point.

• Begin the process of differentiation by

teaching all of your students to do an "anchor activity," which is meaningful work done individually and silently. This could be journal writing, free reading, foreign language pattern drills, seatwork in math, or sketchbook assignments. It's something useful and important for students to do on a relatively regular basis throughout at least a portion of the year. It may seem a bit of a paradox to begin differentiation by *not* differentiating. But when you ask all students to learn to work absolutely quietly on one (or more) anchor activities, you pave the way for breaking off individuals or small groups to do other tasks while the remaining students continue with the comfortable, predictable anchor activity.

• Early on, you may want to ask some students to work with an anchor activity and others to work on a different task, which also requires no conversation or collaboration. This introduces the idea that students won't always do the same work. You create an atmosphere that's conducive to individual focus, and you emphasize attending to one's own work rather than focusing on what someone else does.

• Try a differentiated task for only a small block of time. In a primary classroom, for example, begin a language arts period with all students doing paired reading from the same "reading boxes." After 10 minutes of paired reading, differentiated by reading readiness, call all students to the reading corner to listen to a story together. Now discuss it as a whole class. Or, in a middle school history class, begin with a whole-class discussion and common use of a graphic organizer to compare two time periods. For the last 10 minutes of class, ask students to do one of two journal entries in their learning logs. The entries can be at different levels of complexity or based on two different

interest areas. Starting small like this is the "think-versus-sink" approach. You think your way to success without sinking beneath too many changes. You also teach your students to succeed in an independent, learner-centered class. You don't ask them to manage too many routines and processes for which they are unprepared.

Grow Slowly—but Grow

It's better just to do a few things well. Set goals for yourself, and stick with them, but make sure they are reasonable goals. Like students, teachers grow best when they are moderately challenged. Waiting until conditions are ideal or until you are sure of yourself yields lethargy, not growth. On the other hand, trying to do too many things before you have a chance to think them through leads to frustration and failure. Here are some small but significant starts that might work for you. Pick one or two of them as goals for a year.

• Take notes on your students each day. Be conscious of what works and what doesn't for which learners.

• Assess students before you begin to teach a skill or topic. Study the results of this preassessment and their implications for you and your students.

• Look at all work students do (discussions, journal entries, centers, products, quizzes, group tasks, homework) as indicators of student need, not marks in a gradebook.

• Try creating one differentiated lesson per unit.

• Differentiate one product per semester.

• Find multiple resources for a couple of key parts of your curriculum. For example, consider using several texts, supplementary books at varied readability levels (from basic to quite advanced), videos, or audiotapes that you or volunteers make over time.

• Establish class criteria for success with products. Then work with students to add personal criteria to their lists. You can add one or two for each child based on what you know of the student's strengths and needs.

• Give students more choices about how to work, how to express learning, or which homework assignments to do. (Generally, structured choices work best.)

• Develop and use a two-day learning contract the first marking period, a four-day learning contract the second marking period, and a week-long learning contract the third marking period.

These are just a few possibilities. The idea is to commit yourself to grow. Then try something new, reflect on what you learned from the experience, and apply those insights to the next new step.

Envision How an Activity Will Look

Olympic athletes often pause before an event, close their eyes, and see themselves completing the competition. They envision clearing the vault, making the ski jump, or completing the dive. This is a good idea for a teacher in a differentiated classroom, too. Take time before the day begins to ask yourself how you want a differentiated activity to begin, what you want it to look like as it progresses, and how it should end. Think about what could go wrong along the way. Then plan to keep those things from happening. Write out procedures for yourself and directions you'll give students. Of course you can't envision every possible snafu, but you get better and better at second-guessing and at making plans and giving successful directions. Especially in the early stages, improvisational differentiation is less likely to succeed than choreographed differentiation.

Step Back and Reflect

As you work your way into a differentiated classroom, be sure you think your way into it as well. When you try something new, take time to reflect before you take the next step. You could ask yourself many questions. Here are a few.

• Which students seemed to be engaged in learning? Which were not? Do you know why in either case?

• What evidence do you have that each student understood or "owned" what you hoped would come from the lesson? Do you need to get more evidence to answer this question?

• How did you feel about the introduction you gave to the activity or lesson?

• In what ways did the activity or lesson begin as you wished? Did it get off track? How? What worked and what didn't as students began to work? Were your directions clear? Were materials easily accessible? Did you specify the time for moving (to stations, centers, or small groups, for example)? Did you specify and reinforce the time allotted to settle down?

• As the activity or lesson progressed, how well did students remain focused? If there was point where focus was ragged, can you figure out why? If focus was maintained throughout, why did things work so well? How did group size work? Do any students need to sit in a different place in the room? Did you see any pairings or groups that were unproductive? Were there any students who do not work well in groups, or do not work well alone? Did students know how to monitor the quality of their work? Did they know how to get help?

• How was the conclusion to the activity or lesson? Was there enough warning for students to stop their work in an organized way? Did they know where to put materials and supplies? Were a few students specified to put away materials, move furniture, or handle other clean-up tasks? Were things well organized for the next class or the next day? Did students make the transition to the next class or next activity in a self-controlled way?

• Did you have a sense of who was learning what as the lesson progressed? How did you interact with individuals and groups as they worked? What useful information did you gather as you moved among groups? What effective coaching were you able to do? How might you improve your data gathering and coaching?

Make notes of things you want to retain the next time you try a differentiated activity. Also note things you want to improve. Make specific plans to use the insights you gain from your reflection.

Settling In for the Long Haul

If your teaching philosophy embraces attention to individual students, and if you develop routines and procedures for a differentiated classroom in a systematic and reflective way, differentiation gradually will become a way of life. It won't be something you do every once in a great while. At that point, you need to incorporate at least three things in your routines.

Talk with Students Early and Often

As you develop a clear philosophy about what it means to do differentiated instruction, share your thinking with your students. Be a metacognitive teacher; that is, unpack your thinking in conversations with students. Compared to the images many students have about school, you're changing the "rules." Let them know why and how. Here are some ideas that may help you involve your students in creating a responsive classroom.

• Use an activity that helps students reflect on the fact that they differ from one another in how they learn and what they like to learn about. (They already know this fact quite clearly, by the way.) Depending on the students' ages, the activity will vary. Some teachers ask their students to graph their strengths and weaknesses on a range of skills related and unrelated to the class in question. Some teachers have their students write autobiographies about themselves as learners. They reflect on questions about positive and negative school experiences, best and worst subjects, and effective and ineffective ways of learning. A teacher of young children sent home a survey asking parents to provide ages at which their children sat up, walked, ran, talked, got their first tooth, lost their first tooth, and rode a bike. She helped students create bar graphs that clearly showed how children do things on different timetables. They concluded it wasn't nearly so important when someone learned to talk as it was that they learned. Throughout the year, she brought students back to the graphs to remind them it was fine if some students learned a skill before or after others. In the end, what mattered was learning the skill and using it well.

• When you complete the above activity, let students know that their differing strengths, needs, and learning preferences present an interesting problem to you as a teacher. Ask them if they believe you should pay attention to developing their individual strengths and helping them improve in difficult areas by focusing on the ways that work best for them individually. Or do they believe you will do a better job of teaching by ignoring those things? Chances are, they won't choose the "forget-who-we-are" approach.

• Now you can begin an ongoing discussion of how a differentiated classroom looks and operates. Talk about how your role will differ. For example, you'll work with small groups and individuals rather than only the whole class. Students' roles will differ, too. They'll help and support one another's learning in different ways, making it possible for you to work with individuals and small groups. Students will take more responsibility for class operation, using time wisely so everyone can learn. Their assignments will differ. Not everyone will always have the same assignment in class or for homework. The classroom will look different, with small groups or individuals working on various tasks. Students will see more movement, and they'll use a wider range of materials.

• From this point, you are ready to ask students to help you establish guidelines and procedures to make the classroom work. Let them help you decide how to begin class, how to give directions when multiple things are about to begin at once, how they should get help when you are busy, what they must do when they finish an assignment, how to keep the class focused as activities progress, and how to conclude an activity smoothly. These conversations can occur as the need for each procedure emerges, but they are pivotal in establishing and maintaining a successful learning environment.

Continue to Empower Students

There will always be classroom roles only the teacher can fulfill. However, many teachers have found it easier to do things for students rather than

teach them to do those things for themselves. Look for things you don't have to do, and gradually prepare your students to do them effectively. For example, can students learn to move furniture efficiently and quietly when the room needs to be rearranged? Can students hand out or collect work folders or other materials? Can students check one another's work in a responsible way at any point? Can students learn to straighten up the room? Can they learn to file their own work in designated places rather than bring it to you? Can they learn to keep accurate records of what they complete and when? Can they keep records of their grades to gauge how their performance is progressing? Can they learn to set personal learning goals and to assess their progress according to those goals? The answer to all those questions, and many more like them, is yes—as long as you teach them how! Helping students master these things not only develops more independent and thoughtful learners, but it creates a classroom that belongs to kids as much as to adults. It's also a classroom where the teacher is not frazzled from trying to do everything for everyone!

Continue to Be Analytical

Classrooms are busy places. We often get caught in the undertow of "doing," and we fail to take time for reflecting. Learning to facilitate a differentiated classroom is like learning to conduct a large orchestra. It calls for many players, many parts, many instruments, and many skills. A skilled conductor hears and sees many things at once, but she also takes time away from the podium to reflect on things like the intent of the composer and balance among the sections. She listens to recordings of rehearsals and compares those to performance goals. She identifies a need for additional attention to particular passages and a need for sectional rehearsals.

As your differentiated classroom evolves, cultivate your analytical skills. Some days, just look at how students get into and out of groups, or look only at students who are currently advanced in the subject. Take notes on who elects to work with visual materials and who gravitates to kinesthetic opportunities. Videotape the class every once in a while, or ask a colleague to be a second pair of eyes in your classroom. In either case, you'll identify things that are going well that you'd have missed otherwise, and you'll discover areas that need additional work.

Be analytical with your students, too. Ask them to recall the guidelines you established together for working effectively in a group. Have them analyze with you those procedures that are working well for them and those that are not. Let them make suggestions for how to get even better at working together (or beginning class or moving around the room). Express your pleasure to them when you see them growing in responsibility and independence. Let them tell you when they feel proud. And work together when there is dissonance, too, not to eliminate the passage from the piece, but to attend to it as a whole or in "sectional rehearsals."

Some Practical Considerations

Many years ago, a professor suggested to me that the majority of teaching success stemmed from knowing where to keep the pencils. At the time, I was too much a novice to know what he was saying, and I thought him shallow. Three decades and thousands of students later, I understand. Here are some mundane but altogether essential hints for your consideration as you establish a differentiated classroom. The list is not exhaustive, and some items will not apply to your classroom, but the thoughts below may prompt you to consider something crucial about "where to put the pencils" in your professional world.

Give Thoughtful Directions

When you give directions for multiple tasks simultaneously, don't give everyone directions for all the tasks. It wastes time, it's confusing, and it calls too much attention to task variance. The trick, then, is how to let everyone know what to do without giving whole-group directions. Here are some hints and possibilities:

• Start the class with a familiar task. Once students settle in, meet with one small group at a time to give directions for differentiated tasks.

• Give directions today for tomorrow. That is, today, give directions to a careful listener and a careful follower in each group. They can give directions to their group when the task begins tomorrow.

• Use task cards. Students can go to assigned (or selected) spots in the room and find out what to do by reading a carefully written task card. With younger students, assign more fluent readers to read task cards to the group at the start of the activity.

• Use tape-recorded directions. Tape-recorded directions work wonderfully for students who have difficulty with print, when you don't have time to write a task card, or when directions are complex enough you'd like to explain them a couple of ways.

• Put directions on an overhead or a flip chart for some activities.

• Be sure you think twice about introducing a

completely new format in a small-group task. For example, it makes better sense to use graphic organizers several times with the whole class before you ask a small group to use them. It is better to have all students work at the same learning center until they understand how to work there; then, differentiate work at the center.

• Make yourself "off limits" at strategic times in the instructional sequence. You may want to make it "standard procedure" that no one can ask you questions during the first five minutes of any activity. That way, you can walk among students, making sure they settle down and have their materials. You won't be cornered by one student, giving others the opportunity to remain off task. You also need uninterrupted time for meeting with small groups and individuals. With older students, you just might announce those times. With younger ones, you could indicate you're off limits by wearing a ribbon around your neck or a baseball cap. In either case, make certain students understand why they cannot come to you at those times.

Establish Routines for Getting Help

For a variety of reasons, students in a multitask classroom must learn to get help from someone other than you much of the time. Teach them how to do that, and make provisions for help from other sources.

• Work with students on being good listeners. Kids often learn sloppy listening habits because they know someone will reexplain what they miss. Help them learn to focus on you when you talk, ask them to "replay" what you said in their heads, and ask someone to summarize aloud essential directions. They'll learn to need less help if they listen to you well in the first place. That takes time

on their part and perseverance on yours.

• Ask students to go through a four-step RICE process if they are stuck about what to do next. They first should try hard to **R**ecall what you said. If that doesn't work, they should close their eyes, see you talking, use good practical **I**ntelligence, and **I**magine logically what the directions would have been for the task. If that doesn't help, they can **C**heck with a classmate (someone at their table or nearby doing the same task). This should be done in a whisper. If there's still no sense of direction, designate one or more "**E**xperts of the day" who have the independence or skills necessary to provide guidance. The "expert" should continue with his work, stopping only long enough to help someone who is genuinely stuck. (Over time, most students can serve as an expert of the day for one or more tasks.)

• Make sure students understand that in the rare instances where even the RICE procedure fails, they must then move to a preapproved anchor activity. Let them know it's acceptable to tell you how they tried the RICE procedure, came up empty, and began working with the preapproved alternative until they could get your help. It is not acceptable to sit and wait, or to hinder others. Always be sure students know how much you value time. Help them understand that there are many important things to accomplish and little time for doing them. Wise use of time should be a classroom ethic.

Stay Aware, Stay Organized

Many teachers fear a sense that they will not know what's going on when students work with a variety of tasks in a differentiated classroom. Plus, an effective teacher can't afford to be "out of the loop." In a differentiated classroom, the teacher should have more awareness of what and how students are doing, not less. Teachers must look at the issue of staying "on top of" student progress in a different way. Here are some helpful ideas for accomplishing a new way of staying organized and aware for your classroom.

• Use student work folders. These always stay in the classroom and contain all work in progress (including partially completed tasks, independent study work, and anchor options). The folders also should contain a record-keeping sheet. Here, students document work they have completed and date of completion. Students also should note individual conferences they've had with you, reflecting your conversations about progress and goals. Older students can keep running records of grades on the inside cover of their folders. Such folders provide you a ready way to review student progress and also can be useful for parent-teacher conferences and conferences among parents, teachers, and students.

• Make a list of all skills and competencies you want your students to master in each facet of your subject (for example, in writing, spelling, reading, and grammar). Then extend the list to skills more basic than the ones you're working toward and skills more advanced than the targeted ones. Then turn the skills into a checklist. Sequentially arrange the competencies on the left, and put spaces for several dates and comments across the rest of the page beside each competency. Make one checklist for each student, and keep the lists alphabetically in a notebook. Periodically spot-check students' work using the checklist, or do a formal written or oral assessment with individuals or the group from time to time. As you record observations over time, you should see a clear pattern of individual growth. Not only will that help you monitor student progress, it also should be a great help in developing differentiated assignments targeted to student need. These observations aid in student-teacher planning conferences, too.

• Establish carefully organized and coded places where students should place completed assignments (for example, stack trays, boxes, or folders). This is much more effective than having assignments brought to you, and it is more effective than having a variety of assignments all piled together.

• Carry a clipboard around the class with you much of the time. Make brief notes about nifty things you see students do, "Aha's!", points of confusion, or working conditions that need to be tightened. Use the notes for reflection, planning, and individual and classroom conversations.

• Don't feel compelled to grade everything. (You'd never think of grading a piano student's every practice session!) There's a time for students to figure things out, and a time for seeing if they did, but the two shouldn't always be the same. Help your students see how important it is to complete activities so they become more and more skilled and insightful. Use peer checkers or "experts of the day" when an accuracy check is necessary. When it's time for formal assessment, help students see the link between good practice and success.

• When students are working with sense-making activities and you feel a need to "grade," choose things like whether the student stayed on task, worked hard, got help appropriately, or moved to anchor activities when work was completed. On your clipboard, you might keep a class list with spaces for a daily assessment of these sorts of things. If you see a student have a breakthrough or make a real leap of progress, put a plus in today's space. If a student has real difficulty staying on task despite reminders, put a minus in today's space. Later, put checks in the other spaces. Look for patterns over time, and work with what they tell you. Though you can convert the pattern into a single daily work grade if necessary, there are plenty of other opportunities for formal grading. Remember that grading means more to students if it's infrequent. Continual grading of everything impairs students' willingness to learn from mistakes, makes them teacher dependent, and teaches them to learn for grades, not for its own value. All this grading also makes you crazy and robs you of important thinking and planning time.

Consider "Home Base" Seats

In a differentiated class, it's often helpful to have students assigned to "home base" seats where they begin and end class every day. Students always begin the class in those seats. Some days they will remain in them. If differentiated activities lead them to other parts of the room, they will return to their "home base" seats when the class ends.

"Home base" seats help you check attendance quickly. They make it simple for students to distribute work folders for you. "Home base" seats also make it easier to ensure that the room is straight at the end of an activity, and they provides an orderly format for dismissal or transition. Assigned seats also let you develop positive peer groupings for those times when students work at "home base."

Establish Start-Up and Wrap-Up Procedures

Before students begin to move to various work areas, let them know how quickly they should be in their new places and working. You should make

the time realistic, but you also should be a bit on the stingy side. After students move through the room, let them know how they did. Work with them so they get used to settling in efficiently.

During the activity, keep your eye on the clock. Give students about a two-minute signal that their work time is about to end (flash the lights or just walk to each table and tell them). Follow that with another signal to return to "home base" seating. Students should know that you expect them to return to those seats within 30 seconds.

Teach Students to Work for Quality

A few students in every class seem inclined to measure their success by how quickly they complete their work rather than by how thoughtful they were in doing it. Be clear with your students that craftsmanship and a sense of pride in work are what matter. Help them know why. Let students analyze the differences in work that is hastily finished versus work that shows persistence, revision, and creativity.

Sometimes, students finish work quickly because it's too easy for them or the directions don't clearly state standards of excellence. When those are not problems, patiently and persistently insist that only quality work is acceptable. One teacher called it "working for a Bingo." She taught her students to resist the urge to turn in work until they had done absolutely everything they could think of to improve it. Then they could say, "Bingo! That's it! That's my very best."

Developing a Support System

At least four groups can help you on your path to a differentiated classroom. Colleagues, administrators, parents, and community members all can aid you and your students. With all four groups, you'll probably have to take the initiative to enlist their help. Here are some thoughts about seeking their goodwill and active support.

Calling on Colleagues

The unhappy truth in many schools is that some of your colleagues will be resentful if you do something innovative or expend more energy than the norm in your work. A happier truth is that in these same places, there are always a few soulmates who are energized by their work, catalyzed by someone else's ideas, and ready to take the risk of growth. Find one or two people from the latter group and work together.

In many schools, an art teacher, a special educator, a teacher of the gifted, and a few classroom teachers already differentiate instruction. They may not feel like experts, but neither do you. They have great ideas and routines already in place. You have ideas and questions to enrich them. At the very least, they'll feel enriched by the compliment you pay them in wanting to learn from and with them. Meet with them regularly, ask for time to spend in one another's classrooms, plan together, troubleshoot as a team, share lessons and materials, and take turns teaching and watching as peer coaches. The synergy from such collegial partnerships can be one of the most amazing benefits of a job that all too often is isolating.

Making Principals Partners

Some principals are suspicious of movement and talking in a classroom. I once watched a colleague with whom I team-taught change such an attitude.

This colleague was clear in her own mind about what we were doing in our differentiated classroom and why it was important. She often stopped by the principal's office to say, "When you're out and about in the halls today, you'll notice our students are working in groups." She'd explain why and add, "I hope you'll stop by and take a look." In the beginning, that's what the principal did. He would pause beside the door briefly. My colleague eventually invited, "I hope you'll stop in and watch awhile." When he did that, she encouraged, "Talk with the students and make sure they know what they are doing. I think you'll find that they do." While we taught our students to be resourceful and independent, she taught the principal to appreciate that sort of classroom. He became our biggest champion. If your principal is suspicious of differentiation, or not supportive, for some other reason, try being his or her teacher too!

If your building administrator already supports student-centered, differentiated classrooms, share with him or her your personal goals for the month or the year. Invite your principal to help you figure out how to achieve those goals in your classroom. Your principal then can target observations more appropriately, and you can draw on the insights of a veteran educator who sees lots of classrooms in action.

Bringing Parents Aboard

Most parents want appropriate things for their children in school. They want them to grow, to maximize their strengths and minimize their weaknesses, to find the classroom exciting, and to wake up eager to go to school the next morning. Yet as surely as a differentiated classroom must confront children's images of how we do school, it also must deal with parents' stereotypical images of school.

Ask parents to write out for you, or tell you, their wishes for their child's year in school. Really listen and learn. Then systematically show parents how a differentiated classroom acknowledges and builds on their child's strengths, provides opportunities to bolster weaker areas, keeps track of individual growth, and promotes engagement and excitement. Use a variety of ways to help parents understand that you are building a curriculum and way of instruction that includes the same goals they desire for their youngsters. For example, periodic class letters, weekly or monthly newsletters, parent conferences with work folders or portfolios, and student evaluations help achieve this goal.

You might want to invite parents to take an active role in the class. Parent volunteers can review math concepts with struggling learners, read with advanced readers who want adult conversation about their advanced books, or work on a project with any student who enjoys the pride of knowing an adult finds him worthy of time and attention. Parents also can be a treasure trove of novels, computer expertise, maps, or hands-on learning materials—all things that expand the learning options for their own and others' children.

Parent-teacher partnerships are important to differentiated classrooms. A parent always knows a child more deeply than a teacher possibly can. There's much for the teacher to learn from that depth of knowledge. On the other hand, a teacher knows a child in ways that a parent cannot. There's much for a parent to gain from that breadth of knowledge. Looking at a child from both parent and teacher viewpoints increases the chances of helping that child realize her full potential. The wisest teachers teach parents as

well as children. They eagerly seek opportunities to learn from parents as well.

Involving the Community

The world outside the classroom offers more opportunities than even the most magical classroom. It makes sense to open up a differentiated classroom to that larger world.

Frederick learns best when he builds models of things. Phan needs someone to toss around ideas in his native language before he writes in English. Saranne is more advanced in computers than anyone in her building, and 4th grade Charlie has pretty well finished 6th grade math. Francie desperately wants to know how to dance, Philip is itchy to learn about archeology, and Genice wants to use a 35 mm. camera to take pictures for her history project. The teacher who can facilitate all those things is rare, indeed.

However, a service club can volunteer regularly to make audiotapes for struggling readers and students with learning disabilities. Mentors can help students discover a world of possibilities with photography, baseball statistics, or jazz. A church can provide volunteers for students trying to communicate in two languages. A company can provide old carpet to cover a reading corner in the classroom. Museums and galleries can provide ideas, materials, or guidance on independent projects. A senior citizens center can provide guidance for a wide range of orbital investigations (see Chapter 6). The world is a classroom replete with resources and mentors. A generous teacher links learners with those wide options.

As mentioned before, don't try to do everything at once. Each year, devise one new way to link up with a colleague, gain insight and support from an administrator, learn from and teach parents, or invite a bit of the world into your classroom. Remember that becoming an expert at differentiation is a career-long goal. One step at a time, you can get there.

When Educational Leaders Seek Differentiated Classrooms

10

> It is so easy to underestimate the complexities of the change process . . . . Change is difficult because it is riddled with dilemmas, ambivalences, and paradoxes. It combines steps that do not seem to go together: to have a clear vision and be open-minded; to take initiative and empower others; to provide support and pressure; to start small and think big; to expect results and be patient and persistent; to have a plan and be flexible; to use top-down and bottom-up strategies; to experience uncertainty and satisfaction.
> Michael G. Fullan with Suzanne Stiegelbauer
> *The New Meaning of Educational Change*

Differentiating instruction is not an instructional strategy or a teaching model. It's a way of thinking about teaching and learning that advocates beginning where individuals are rather than with a prescribed plan of action, which ignores student readiness, interest, and learning profile. It is a way of thinking that challenges how educators typically envision assessment, teaching, learning, classroom roles, use of time, and curriculum.

Individual teachers who feel a need to take up this challenge can read a book like this one, meld its philosophies with their practice, and reshape their classrooms. Often, however, other educational leaders see a need for change on a broader scale. This chapter addresses department chairs, principals, and district-level administrators who want to be catalysts for developing differentiated classrooms. The chapter is predicated on the belief that while school change is difficult, it is more likely to occur if it is rooted in the best current knowledge of the change process. This is a vital understanding because schools embark on a path of significant change when they begin to develop differentiated classrooms.

Experience, Research, and School Change

We know much about the change process in education: what supports and undermines it, its stages, and the roles and responses of various participants. The scope of this chapter is not adequate even to summarize the work of researchers like Michael Fullan (e.g., 1993), Seymour Sarason (e.g., 1990, 1993), and others whose insights have illuminated a murky process. Nonetheless, key conclusions from their work supports the advice below.

The headings that follow reflect some essential principles for guiding change in schools. This is not meant to be linear advice. Change is complex, messy, and unpredictable. When we undertake change, we start, we start over, and we even skip steps. Yet the following suggestions are important for reflection, over time, as a school or district leader guides change leading to differentiated classrooms.

Examine Your Beliefs and Goals

Spend time thinking about why the idea of differentiated classrooms is sensible and important to you. Is it because you believe profoundly in the importance of effective heterogeneous communities of learning for the future of U.S. public schools and society? Is it because you see too many students disenchanted with standardized classes? Is

it because of what you know about cognitive psychology and how the brain works? Is it because you want to save money? Not all motivations are equal.

You must know why you think it's worth the trouble to create differentiated classes. You must be able to articulate your viewpoint clearly and believably to those you lead. If you do not have a compelling sense of why differentiated classrooms are worthwhile, you would be wise to move *away* from differentiation as a focus of your leadership.

Establish and Share a Vision

Leadership has a great deal to do with creating a vision and inspiring others to join you in working to achieve it. What might classrooms in your school or district look like if change occurs? Why would that be positive? For whom?

Don't ask teachers to do something shrouded in uncertainty. Be sure you are clear on your definitions of and goals for differentiation. Explain these definitions and goals so others can examine them and talk with you about them. Then do a difficult thing: Hold the vision with one hand and reach out with the other to invite other leaders, teachers, and parents to revise and extend that vision. It is a paradox of change that leaders must believe in their ideas but be open to the reality that others must reshape those ideas for change to truly happen.

The goal is clear: You want to foster classrooms where excellent teaching is targeted to the variable learning needs of diverse students. This book offers one way to think about reaching that goal. There are other ways to think about it. Remain open to all ideas, and invite other stakeholders to help you think more broadly. Initiating change begins with sharing a sense of direction, but you also must understand that few worthwhile journeys progress in a straight line.

Avoid Overload

Teachers often perceive that they are asked to learn and apply many disparate skills simultaneously. They feel discouraged if they sense that differentiated classrooms are "just one more thing to do." To that end, it's vital to avoid a feeling of "overload" among teachers.

To plant the seeds for effective change, leaders first need to focus on one key goal, such as making classrooms more responsive to the full range of learners. Ensure that the goal remains central in everyone's thinking. As much as possible, defer initiatives that impede attention to that goal. Present initiatives that help achieve the goal in that context. For example, tell staff members, "We are learning about literature circles because they help us attend to differences in student readiness and interests in the following ways." Or, tell them, "Learning about cultural and gender patterns can help us achieve our goals of responsive classrooms in the following ways."

Prepare for the Long Haul

Substantial change is a slow process that must be initiated, implemented, and institutionalized. It almost inevitably requires 5 to 10 years. If you are serious about crafting differentiated classrooms, make a time line and plan of that duration. Let others know the idea is "here to stay" by publishing essentials of the plan and time line so they can take the long look with you. Of course, the plan will be reshaped over time, and the time line will be revised. But you should demonstrate an unshakable commitment to the duration required to make meaningful change.

Educators have a destructive habit of ballyhooing the fad of the year, or even of the month, and then backing off. All teachers know that if they lay low for a while, whatever pesky initiative they'd like to avoid will vanish. There is no quick-fix to making differentiation a reality. Making differentiation a one-year goal dooms the idea to failure, and it diminishes the chance that your colleagues will ever really do what is required to change anything in schools.

Start Smart

Several characteristics typify the start of smart change. Consider these.

• Begin small. Try a few pilot teachers and classrooms rather than a whole school (and rather than a whole district).

• Begin with teachers who have the skill and will to change. These teachers are already reflective about their practice, sensitive to their students, flexible in their instructional patterns, and ready to learn. This will yield early successes, strategies for dealing with inevitable problems, and a cadre of teachers who can become staff developers as the process expands.

• Create teams of teachers who can work together, share ideas and materials, troubleshoot with one another, coteach, or observe one another and provide feedback. Collegiality, not isolation, is far more nourishing to new ideas.

• Go for action and application. It's extremely important for teachers to think about their beliefs as change occurs. For example, implementing a new approach to teaching math without a sense of how that fits into the larger picture of learning is likely to result in an ill-used strategy. Teaching makes pragmatists of teachers. They are more likely to change their beliefs because of something they successfully implement in their classrooms; they won't necessarily try a new approach just because they have changed their beliefs.

Model the Process of Differentiation

In a differentiated classroom, a teacher says something like this to students: "Here's where we're headed. That we all learn and grow and work hard in the process is not negotiable. How we reach the destination is. Some of us may move more rapidly than others. Some begin further ahead. Some may succeed better with Plan A, others with Plan B. Sometimes I as teacher will make some decisions. Sometimes you as students will make them. Often we will make them together. We will always try to make them in ways that help us all achieve the goal of maximum growth."

When they begin an initiative like differentiated instruction, educational leaders take on the teacher role. They must realize that schools and teachers differ. That they all make progress toward the goal of differentiated classrooms is not negotiable. How they get there is. Different schools and various teachers have differing readiness levels, interests, and learning profiles. They will need to develop the process of differentiation on different time tables, through different routes, and with differing forms of assistance. Sometimes leaders will make key decisions. Sometimes teachers must make them. Often they need to be made jointly—and always with an eye to maximizing progress toward differentiated classrooms. Leaders who model differentiation exemplify the kind of respectful environment needed in responsive classrooms. Leaders and models also provide natural opportunities to talk with colleagues about how differentiation works.

Examine Policies and Procedures

Often, leaders ask teachers to accomplish objectives even though national, state, district, and local policies and procedures make it difficult to do so. Sometimes leaders need to modify these policies and procedures to support differentiation.

• Adjust school schedules to provide teachers larger blocks of uninterrupted time. It is difficult to set up and carry out a differentiated science lab in a 40-minute class period.

• Should your district consider adopting multiple texts rather than one text for a given subject and grade level? A district that provides the same reading book for all 3rd graders sends a message that differentiation may not be so important.

• Should your district plan for modified report cards that help parents and students look at personal growth instead of, or in addition to, comparison to a group? Report cards that are all about sorting students make it difficult for teachers to conceive how to grade students in differentiated classrooms.

• Should your school consider narrowing the range of learners in some classrooms? Teaching in Noah's Ark with two of every kind of learner in the school population may not be the most encouraging or efficient early approach to student assignment for all teachers, while homogeneous grouping is often not the best solution for establishing equitable communities of learning. In the early stages of differentiation, however, teachers may be overextended by trying to address every sort of learning need in one classroom.

• In what innovative ways can you reduce class size, find more helpers, or increase classroom space for teachers willing to significantly differentiate instruction (at least in the early stages of teacher learning)?

• Do you need to communicate with parents about differentiation from a school or district level? Or do you expect teachers alone to educate parents about the approach, its potential benefits to students, and opportunities for participation?

Sometimes, leaders can't change things; they only can help teachers rethink particular policies or procedures. For example, many teachers see the emphasis on high-stakes testing as contradictory to attending to student differences. Actually, dragging all students through the same material whether they are academically ahead or behind, at a speed that is unrealistically fast for most and too slow for some, and in the same teacher-dominated mode has never yielded a set of ideal scores. It certainly has never generated a group of stimulated and excited learners.

Top-down benchmarks or standards shouldn't "become" the curriculum, but they can be incorporated into lessons that engage students. Helping teachers see the difference, and giving them the freedom to take the more engaging approach, is essential to making differentiated classrooms a reality. A district-level leader who sends the message that teachers' success depends on their capacity to get everyone to score "above average" on a test should not also mandate differentiated classrooms.

Plan Staff Development for the Complexity of Change

Early in the process of change, it is useful to have staff development sessions where

differentiation is defined, discussed, and illustrated. If such sessions are a match with school or district definitions, principles, and goals—and if they are convincingly presented—they can be a part of effective orientation to an idea. Continued "frontal" presentations, however, rapidly lose their power to generate action. Figure 10.1 presents a model for a more realistic approach to staff development around the ideas of differentiated classrooms.

There is a time when teachers need new information about a topic: concepts, principles, skills. That may be accomplished through staff development presentations, reading, watching videos, or individual and small-group inquiry. Then, however, teachers need time and opportunity to make sense of the new ideas. Leaders must provide time and structures that promote teacher reflection on the ideas. Teachers must set long-term and short-term personal goals for translating the ideas into classroom action. They also must make specific implementation plans. Sometimes it will be helpful for teachers to plan in pairs, to arrange for coteaching or peer observation, and later to arrange peer debriefing.

At that point, based on what they learned from the translation attempt (including self-reflection, peer input, and student feedback), teachers may be ready for additional information, help with polishing the skill they attempted, or exposure to another procedure, with additional responsive input. Here again, the staff development cycle is much like good teaching in the classroom. Staff developers must

• know essential facts, concepts, principles, and skills necessary to attain desired outcomes;

• develop a sequence of presenting them or having the learners encounter them;

Figure 10.1
Becoming Practitioners of Differentiation

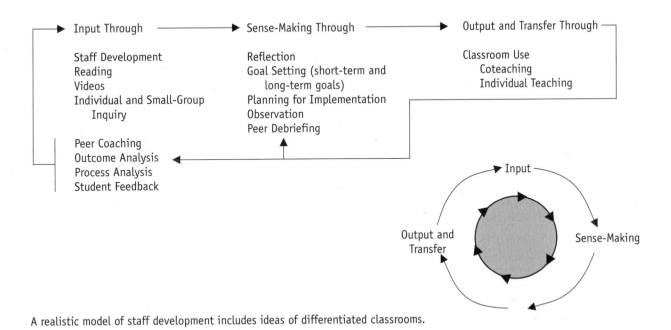

A realistic model of staff development includes ideas of differentiated classrooms.

• assess learner readiness for mastering them;

• provide opportunities for learners to make sense of and try out the new ideas; and

• tailor the next learning opportunity to the current learning status of the learner.

Remember to think through the various continuums on which learners differ. Some may have the skill to conceive sound differentiated instruction but lack the will to do so. Some may have the will but lack the skill to think about their curriculum in a new way. Some can handle a new approach to curriculum but stumble when it comes to setting up a student-centered classroom. Others already may have a student-centered classroom but find it difficult to work with a concept-based approach to learning. Some, but not all, will need guidance in developing a new belief system. One-size-fits-all staff development is wrong for work on differentiated classrooms. Staff development is another important opportunity to model what you believe.

Provide Ongoing Assistance

Throughout the long change cycle, teachers will need sustained support. They need leaders to help them by

• making time to plan differentiated lessons;

• creating differentiated curriculums when curriculum guides are revised;

• providing opportunities to visit differentiated classrooms;

• giving access to a wide range of learner materials;

• making them feel safe in trying a new approach in their classrooms, with no fear of judgment if there is noise or clutter for awhile;

• giving meaningful, targeted feedback about their work with differentiation;

• providing networks of mutual support and encouragement for teachers who are early subscribers to the initiative so they do not feel alone if they are "punished" by colleagues who resist the change; and

• expressing clear appreciation when they have done a good job, or even taken a risk that was less than successful.

Effective leaders continue to look for ways to support and sustain teacher efforts. They do not send teachers into uncharted territory alone.

Apply Pressure and Offer Support

Classrooms invite inertia. Too many students have too many needs and require too many interactions each day. Much about schools and classrooms makes it easy to resist change, to wait for a "better day" to try differentiating instruction. I once heard a speaker say that teachers change either because they see the light or because they feel the heat. Change researchers have concluded that both are necessary for change.

Effective administrators are sources of both light and heat. They help teachers see the benefits of new initiatives while simultaneously insisting on progress. Teacher leaders such as subject area coordinators, grade-level chairs, and special education teachers are good sources of light, but generally they have no capacity to apply heat. They should not feel ineffective because of this. Instead, they must be supported with heat by those whose positions allow them to generate it.

Link Differentiation to Professional Responsibility

While the term "differentiating instruction" may be new, the idea of tailoring a service to meet a client's needs is not. Even in education, where clients arrive in batches of 20 to 30 at a time, teachers learn early that individuals are not alike and do not "get" what's presented in lock-step fashion. While many teachers do not practice active differentiation, most hold fast to the belief that it is the teacher's role to address individual needs (e.g., Tomlinson, Callahan, Moon, Tomchin, Landrum, Imbeau, Hunsaker, & Eiss, 1995).

Helping teachers develop an understanding of their professional responsibility to engage each individual in meaningful and powerful learning is at the core of moving toward differentiated classrooms. Charlotte Danielson (1996) developed a framework for thinking about teacher development in four key domains of teaching: planning and preparation, classroom environment, instruction, and professional responsibilities (such as communicating with families, reflecting on teaching, growing professionally, and contributing to the school and district). In each domain, she proposes standards and benchmarks at levels of performance she calls unsatisfactory, basic, proficient, and distinguished.

Throughout the rich and extensive framework, distinguished performance is marked by responsiveness to students' varying needs (see Figure 10.2, pp. 116–117). While the framework is not intended to overlay with differentiated instruction, it reflects the reality that a hallmark of excellent teachers is their capacity to see and serve individuals rather than batches of children.

Using a framework such as Danielson's can help teachers plan to reach individual learners, reflect upon their efforts, and receive guided peer feedback regarding their developing skills. Further, such benchmarks can become part of a teacher assessment procedure through which teachers set personal goals for responsive teaching, work toward those goals, and receive targeted feedback from leaders who support their progress. Such an approach should be a source of both light and heat, with insight about implementation and accountability.

A Word About Novice Teachers

The quality of tomorrow's classrooms rests squarely on today's preparation of the next generation of teachers. Research suggests that teacher education programs too often fall short of preparing preservice teachers for the inevitability of academically diverse classrooms (Tomlinson, Callahan, Tomchin, Eiss, Imbeau, & Landrum, 1997). For example, in the study cited, preservice teachers:

• Seldom, if ever, experienced differentiated instruction in their teacher preparation programs.

• Generally had only one survey course about exceptional children to help them understand the needs of academically diverse learners. Almost without exception, the preservice teachers reported that the class dealt exclusively with learner traits and offered little memorable guidance in "what to do with them."

• Were almost never encouraged to actively differentiate instruction by education professors, university supervisors, or master teachers.

• Were often discouraged from differentiation, particularly by master teachers who encouraged them to "keep everyone together."

• Had few instructional strategies with which they felt comfortable. Thus, they had a shallow well of options for addressing students' diverse needs.

• Had few, if any, images of multitask classrooms to carry with them into their first teaching assignments.

Once in their own classrooms, the undertow for new teachers to "teach to the middle" is profound, both because of the complexity of teaching and because of peer pressure to conform to "the way we do school here." The few novice teachers who had master teachers who differentiated instruction were far more likely to do so in their first teaching placements than their classmates.

Early teaching is a time to develop the "gross motor skills" of the profession. Robust differentiation is a "fine motor skill" of teaching. Thus, few novice teachers will display great proficiency in planning and facilitating fully differentiated classrooms, and they should not be expected to do so. Nonetheless, there is a need to help novices develop the "gross motor skills" that ultimately will evolve into the "fine motor skills" of responsive teaching.

Teacher education programs and school districts that employ novice teachers should:

• Set clear expectations for the novice's growth in student-centered, responsive instruction.

• Provide clear models of differentiated curriculum and differentiated instruction in action.

• Provide mentoring that helps teachers reflect on student needs and appropriate responses to those needs.

• Ensure teachers' comfort in implementing a growing range of instructional strategies that invite differentiation and facilitate its management.

• Provide early partnerships with teachers who practice differentiation.

Figure 10.2
Differentiation as a Professional Responsibility

Element of Professional Practice	Characteristic of Distinguished Performance	Link with Differentiating Instruction
Knowledge of relationships among content elements	Teacher's plans and practices reflect knowledge of the relationships among topics and concepts. Teacher uses this knowledge to seek causes for student misunderstanding.	• concept-based instruction • ongoing assessment
Knowledge of characteristics of age group	Teacher displays knowledge of typical development characteristics of age group, exceptions to patterns, and extent to which each student follows patterns.	• focus on individual learners
Knowledge of students' varied approaches to learning	Teacher uses, where appropriate, knowledge of students' varied approaches to learning in instructional planning.	• learning profile
Knowledge of students' skills and knowledge	Teacher displays knowledge of each student's skills and knowledge, including knowledge of special needs.	• readiness
Knowledge of students' interests and cultural heritage	Teacher displays knowledge of the interests or cultural heritage of each student.	• interest • learning profile
Suitability of planning and preparation for diverse students	Goals take into account the varying needs of individual students or groups.	• responsive instruction

Figure 10.2—*continued*
Differentiation as a Professional Responsibility

Element of Professional Practice	Characteristic of Distinguished Performance	Link with Differentiating Instruction
Instructional groups	Instructional groups are varied, as appropriate to the different instructional goals. There is evidence of student choice in selecting different patterns of instructional groups.	• flexible grouping
Lesson and unit structure	The lesson or unit structure is clear and allows for different pathways according to student needs.	• focused instruction • different pathways to learning
Teacher and student interaction	Teacher demonstrates genuine caring and respect for individual students. Students exhibit respect for the teacher as an individual and as a teacher. Students demonstrate genuine caring for others as individuals and students.	• learning triangle • community of learning
Instructional persistence	Teacher persists in seeking effective approaches for students who need help, using an extensive repertoire of strategies, and soliciting additional resources from the school.	• use of a wide range of instructional strategies • use of varied text and supplementary materials
Lesson adjustment	Teacher successfully makes a major adjustment to a lesson (in response to student needs).	• differentiated content or process

Based on *Frameworks for Teaching,* C. Danielson, ASCD, 1997.

• Provide time and structure for reflecting on and planning for student needs.

• Recognize growth toward responsive instruction in meaningful ways.

As schools become increasingly diverse, their capacity to provide a meaningful and empowering education for all individuals is directly related to our willingness to invest the time, resources, and guidance needed for beginning teachers to move away from teach-to-the-middle instruction. We must help them move toward teaching that meets individuals at their points of readiness, interest, and learning profile.

For More Information

For additional information on the change process as it specifically relates to differentiation,

Tomlinson, C. (1995). Deciding to differentiate instruction in middle school: One school's journey. *Gifted Child Quarterly, 39,* 77-87.

A Final Thought

For most teachers like me, the classroom is the place where we spend our entire careers. For 25 or 30 years, we mark the days and seasons with entering and leaving the solitary yet crowded room in which we learn and practice our profession. The classroom is the place where we give the better part of our lifetimes trying to make a difference.

It is a curiosity of teaching that no two days are alike, but, if we are not careful, all the days can take on a deadening sameness. We must remember that we have every opportunity to transform ourselves and our practice, just as we have every opportunity to stagnate, remaining much the same teachers we were when we began.

The ideas presented in this book are ambitious, maybe even visionary. They also are well within the reach of teachers who seek daily to do what we ought to ask of all students: risk, stretch, push a bit beyond a comfort zone.

Lewis Thomas (1983) suggests that as a human race, we need to celebrate our ignorance rather than pretend we have many answers to life's complexities. "We can take some gratification at having come a certain distance," he says, "but it should be a deeper satisfaction, even an exhilaration, to realize we still have such a distance to go" (p. 163).

So it is with teaching, and that is the spirit of this book: neither to mourn what we have not done nor to rest on our victories, but to look at all the reasons we have to show up again tomorrow at the classroom door, ready to join our students—all of our students—in learning.

Appendix

Two Models to Guide Differentiated Instruction

Figure A.1 is a model for thinking about how to differentiate instruction in academically diverse classrooms. It emphasizes differentiation by student readiness. The model is discussed more fully in the sources cited at the end of Chapter 2.

In brief, the model suggests that all **content** for all learners should demonstrate the characteristics in the box on the top left. **Processes**, or activities, for all students should demonstrate the characteristics in the top center box. **Product** assignments for all students should demonstrate the characteristics in the box on the top right. All students should experience learning environments with the characteristics listed around the perimeter of the box.

The lower row of boxes contains sample instructional strategies to help teachers achieve differentiated content, process, and product. These strategies, too, are useful with all students. While these lists are not exhaustive, they reflect a current understanding of best educational practice.

The "buttons" beneath the two rows of boxes are drawn to look like a stereo or CD player's buttons, which listeners slide to adjust tone, volume, and balance. Such mechanisms are called "equalizers." To differentiate for learner readiness, a teacher should begin with solid, focused, significant instruction. Then the teacher should move the equalizer buttons toward the left or right, based on a learner's starting point. For example, a learner who knows a great deal about outer space and who reads quite well might need to use complex research materials to prepare for tomorrow's presentation. A classmate who doesn't read well and whose background knowledge is less extensive may need to use simpler research materials to prepare for the presentation.

As with a stereo, it is not necessary to move all the buttons at the same time. Also, students may need several equalizer buttons pushed toward the left when they begin work on a topic or skill, but as a unit progresses, their activities and products should reflect movement of the buttons toward the right.

Figure A.2, "Thinking About the Equalizer," provides some descriptors to help teachers and curriculum developers consider ways to modify curriculum and instruction along various continuums. For example, if a learner is struggling with a particular idea or skill, a teacher may want to design a task that is foundational, or basic, for that child.

Figure A.1
A Planning Model for Academic Diversity and Talent Development

Flexible Grouping

Active Orientation ———→

Content	Process	Product
Concept and generalization-based High relevance Coherent Transferable Powerful Authentic	Concept and generalization driven Focused High level Purposeful Balancing critical and creative thought Promoting cognition and metacognition	Concept or issue centered Skills of planning taught Skills of production taught Requires application of all key skills and understandings Uses skills of the discipline Real problems and audiences Multiple modes of expression
<u>Differentiation through</u> Multiple texts and supplementary print resources Varied computer programs Varied audio-visuals Varied support mechanisms Varied time allotments Interest centers Contracts Compacting Triarchic-based orientation Complex instruction Group investigation	<u>Differentiation through</u> Tiered assignments Learning centers Triarchic model assignments Multiple intelligences assignments Graphic organizers Simulation Learning logs Concept attainment Concept development Synectics Complex instruction Group investigation	<u>Differentiation through</u> Tiered product assignments Independent study Community-based products Negotiated criteria Graduated rubrics Triarchic-based orientations Multiple intelligences-based orientations Complex instruction Group investigation

Escalating Expectation ———→

1. Foundational  Transformational

Information, Ideas, Materials, Applications

2. Concrete  Abstract

Representations, Ideas, Applications, Materials

Figure A.1—*continued*
A Planning Model for Academic Diversity and Talent Development

Continual Assessment and Adaptation
The Equalizer

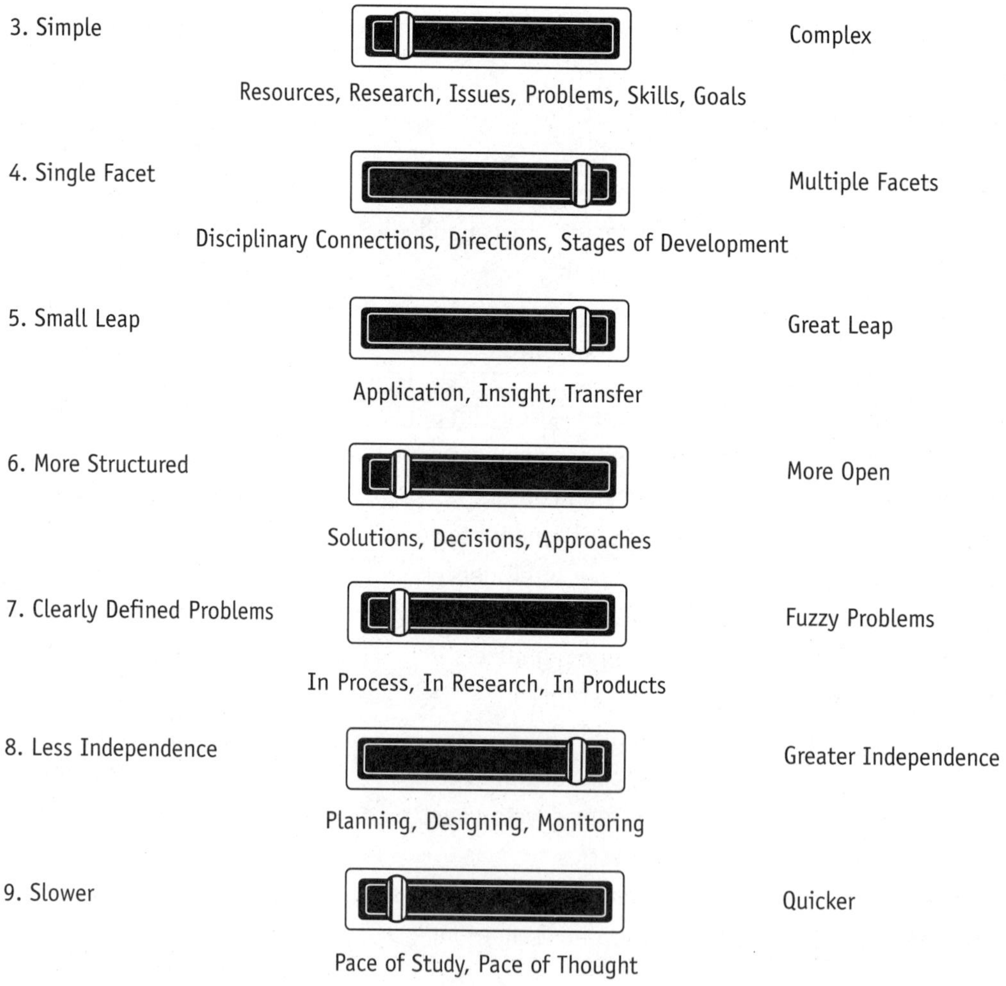

3. Simple   Complex

Resources, Research, Issues, Problems, Skills, Goals

4. Single Facet   Multiple Facets

Disciplinary Connections, Directions, Stages of Development

5. Small Leap   Great Leap

Application, Insight, Transfer

6. More Structured   More Open

Solutions, Decisions, Approaches

7. Clearly Defined Problems   Fuzzy Problems

In Process, In Research, In Products

8. Less Independence   Greater Independence

Planning, Designing, Monitoring

9. Slower   Quicker

Pace of Study, Pace of Thought

Figure A.2
Thinking About the Equalizer

1. Foundational ▭ Transformational

Information, Ideas, Materials, Applications

-close to text or experience	-removed from text or experience
-expert idea and skill to similar or familiar setting	-export idea or skill to unexpected or unfamiliar setting
-use key idea or skill alone	-use key idea or skill with unrelated idea or skill
-fundamental skills and knowledge emphasized	-use but move beyond fundamental skills and knowledge
-fewer permutations of skills and ideas	-more permutations of skills and ideas

2. Concrete ▭ Abstract

Representations, Ideas, Applications, Materials

-hold in hands or hands-on	-hold in mind or minds on
-tangible	-intangible
-literal	-symbolic or metaphorical
-physical manipulation	-mental manipulation
-event based	-idea based
-event to principle	-principle without event
-demonstrated and explained	-not demonstrated or explained

3. Simple ▭ Complex

Resources, Research, Issues, Problems, Skills, Goals

-use idea or skill being taught	-combine idea or skill being taught with those previously taught
-work with no one, or few abstractions	-work with multiple abstractions
-emphasizes appropriateness	-emphasizes elegance
-requires relatively less originality	-requires relatively more originality
-more common vocabulary	-more advanced vocabulary
-more accessible readability	-more advanced readability

4. Single Facet ▭ Multiple Facets

Disciplinary Connections, Directions, Stages of Development

-fewer parts	-more parts
-fewer steps	-more steps
-fewer stages	-more stages

5. Small Leap ▭ Great Leap

Application, Insight, Transfer

-few unknowns	-many unknowns
-relative comfort with most elements	-relative unfamiliarity with many elements
-less need to change familiar elements	-more need to change familiar elements
-requires less flexible thought	-requires more flexible thought
-few gaps in required knowledge	-significant gaps in required knowledge
-more evolutionary	-more revolutionary

6. More Structured ▭ More Open

Solutions, Decisions, Approaches

-more directions or more precise directions	-fewer directions
-more modeling	-less modeling
-relatively less student choice	-relatively more student choice

7. Clearly Defined Problems ▭ Fuzzy Problems

In Process, In Research, In Products

-few unknowns	-more unknowns
-more algorithmic	-more heuristic
-narrower range of acceptable responses or approaches	-wider range of acceptable responses or approaches
-only relevant data provided	-extraneous data provided
-problem specified	-problem unspecified or ambiguous

8. Less Independence ▭ Greater Independence

Planning, Designing, Monitoring

-more teacher or adult guidance and monitoring on	-less teacher or adult guidance and monitoring on
• problem identification	• problem identification
• goal setting	• goal setting
• establishing timelines	• establishing timelines
• following timelines	• following timelines
• securing resources	• securing resources
• use of resources	• use of resources
• criteria for success	• criteria for success
• formulation of a product	• formulation of a product
• evaluation	• evaluation
-more teacher scaffolding	-less teacher scaffolding
-learning the skills of independence	-demonstrating the skills of independence

9. Slower ▭ Quicker

Pace of Study, Pace of Thought

-more time to work	-less time to work
-more practice	-less practice
-more teaching and reteaching	-less teaching and reteaching
-process more systematically	-process more rapidly
-probe breadth and depth	-hit the high points

Students may make the necessary mental connections or applications when they are asked to work with an idea or skill in a way that is largely like text or class examples, or that is familiar in their own experiences. A child in the same classroom who already is comfortable with an idea or skill may need to and be ready to apply it in a way that is transformational, that is, removed from text and class examples or removed from personal experience.

These lists of descriptors also are not exhaustive. It's a good reflective exercise to think about what you do to make tasks appropriate for the varied learners in your classroom. Then add to these lists the descriptors that reflect your way of thinking about differentiation based on student readiness.

Bibliography

Allan, S. (1991). Ability-grouping research reviews: What do they say about grouping and the gifted? *Educational Leadership, 48*(6), 60–65.

Arnow, H. (1954). *The dollmaker.* New York: Avon.

Barell, J. (1995). *Teaching for thoughtfulness: Classroom strategies to enhance intellectual development.* White Plains, NY: Longman.

Bauer, J. (1996). *Sticks.* New York: Yearling.

Bauer, J. (1997). *Sticks:* Between the lines. *Book Links, 6*(6), 9–12.

Berliner, D. (1986). In pursuit of the expert pedagogue. *Educational Researcher, 15*(7), 5–13.

Berte, N. (1975). *Individualizing education by learning contracts.* San Francisco: Jossey-Bass.

Bess, J. (Ed.). (1997). *Teaching well and liking it: Motivating faculty to teach effectively.* Baltimore, MD: The Johns Hopkins University Press.

Bluestein, J. (Ed.). (1995). *Mentors, masters and Mrs. MacGregor: Stories of teachers making a difference.* Deerfield Beach: FL: Health Communications, Inc.

Brandwein, P. (1981). *Memorandum: On renewing schooling and education.* New York: Harcourt Brace Jovanovich.

Brown, M. (1949). *The important book.* New York: Harper and Row.

Caine, R., & Caine, G. (1991). *Making connections: Teaching and the human brain.* Alexandria, VA: ASCD.

Caine, R., & Caine, G. (1994). *Making connections: Teaching and the human brain* (Rev. ed.). Menlo Park, CA: Addison-Wesley.

Caine, R., & Caine, G. (1997). *Education on the edge of possibility.* Alexandria, VA: ASCD.

Canter & Associates. (1996). *Teaching strategies that promote organization and mastery of content.* [From Developing Lifelong Learners Video Series.] Santa Monica, CA: Author.

Clemons, J., Laase, L., Cooper, D., Areglado, N., & Dill, M. (1993). *Portfolios in the classroom: A teacher's sourcebook.* New York: Scholastic.

Cohen, E. (1994). *Designing groupwork: Strategies for the heterogeneous classroom* (2nd ed.). New York: Teachers College Press.

Csikszentmihalyi, M., Rathunde, K., & Whalen, S. (1993). *Talented teenagers: The roots of success and failure.* New York: Cambridge University Press.

Danielson, C. (1996). *Enhancing professional practice: A framework for teaching.* Alexandria, VA: ASCD.

Danielson, C., & Abrutyn, L. (1997). *An introduction to using portfolios in the classroom.* Alexandria, VA: ASCD.

Delisle, R. (1997). *How to use problem-based learning in the classroom.* Alexandria, Va.: ASCD.

Eisner, E. (1994). *Cognition and curriculum reconsidered.* New York: Teacher's College Press.

Erikson, H. (1998). *Concept-based curriculum and instruction: Teaching beyond the facts.* Thousand Oaks, CA: Corwin.

Fleischman, P. (1996). *Dateline Troy.* Cambridge, MA: Candlewick Press.

Fullan, M. G. & Stiegelbauer, S. (1991). *The new meaning of educational change.* New York: Teachers College Press.

Fullan, M. (1993). *Change forces: Probing the depths of educational reform.* Bristol, PA: The Falmer Press.

Gardner, H. (1991). *The unschooled mind. How children think and how schools should teach.* New York: Basic Books.

Gardner, H. (1993). *Multiple intelligences: The theory in practice.* New York: Basic Books.

Gardner, H. (1997). Reflections on multiple intelligences: Myths and messages. *Phi Delta Kappan, 78*(5), 200–207.

Horowitz, F., & O'Brien, M. (1985). *The gifted and talented: Developmental perspectives.* Washington, DC: American Psychological Association.

Howard, P. (1994). *The owner's manual for the brain.* Austin, TX: Leornian Press.

Jensen, E. (1998). *Teaching with the brain in mind.* Alexandria, VA: ASCD.

Johnson, T. (Producer). (1997). *Problem-based learning.* [Videotape and facilitator's guide.] Alexandria, VA: Association for Supervision and Curriculum Development.

Kalbfleisch, L. (1997). *Explain the brain.* Unpublished manuscript. Charlottesville, VA: University of Virginia.

Kaplan, S., Kaplan, J., Madsen, S., & Gould, B. (1980). *Change for children: Ideas and activities for individualizing learning.* Glenview, IL: Scott Foresman.

Kiernan, L. (producer) (1997). *Differentiating instruction: A video staff development set.* Alexandria, VA: ASCD.

Kingore, B. (1993). *Portfolios.* Des Moines, IA: Leadership Publishers.

Knowles, M. (1986). *Using learning contracts.* San Francisco: Jossey-Bass.

Konigsburg, E. L. (1996). *The view from Saturday.* New York: Atheneum Books for Young Readers.

Kulik, J., & Kulik, C. (1991). Ability grouping and gifted students. In N. Colangelo and G. Davis (Eds.), *Handbook of Gifted Education* (pp. 178–196). Boston: Allyn & Bacon.

Lasley, T. J., & Matczynski, T. J. (1997). *Strategies for teaching in a diverse society: Instructional models.* Belmont, CA: Wadsworth Publishing Company.

Lowry, L. (1993). *The giver.* Boston: Houghton Mifflin.

Madea, B. (1994). *The multiage classroom: An inside look at one community of learners.* Cypress, CA: Creative Teaching Press.

McCarthy, B. (1996). *About learning.* Barrington, IL: Excel.

Oakes, J. (1985). *Keeping track: How schools structure inequality.* New Haven, CT: Yale University Press.

Ohanian, S. (1988). On stir-and-serve recipes for teaching. In K. Ryan & J. M. Cooper (Eds.), *Kaleidoscope: Readings in education* (pp. 56–61). Boston: Allyn & Bacon.

Paterson, K. (1991). *Lyddie.* New York: Dutton.

Phenix, P. (1986). *Realms of meaning: A philosophy of the curriculum for general education.* Ventura, CA: Ventura County Superintendent of Schools Office.

Reis, S., & Renzulli, J. (1992). Using curriculum compacting to challenge the above average. *Educational Leadership, 50*(2), 51–57.

Robb, L. (1997). Talking with Paul Fleischman. *Book Links, 6*(4), 39–43.

Saint Exupery, A. (1943). *The little prince.* New York: Harcourt, Brace & World.

Sarason, S. (1990). *The predictable failure of educational reform: Can we change course before it's too late?* San Francisco: Jossey-Bass.

Sarason, S. (1993). *The case for change: Rethinking the preparation of educators.* San Francisco: Jossey-Bass.

Schiever, S. (1991). *A comprehensive approach to teaching thinking.* Boston: Allyn & Bacon.

Sharan, S. (Ed.). (1994). *Handbook of cooperative learning methods.* Westport, CT: Greenwood Press.

Sharan, Y., & Sharan, S. (1992). *Expanding cooperative learning through group investigation.* New York: Teachers College Press.

Siegel, J., & Shaughnessy, M. (1994). Educating for understanding: A conversation with Howard Gardner. *Phi Delta Kappan, 75*(7), 564.

Sizer, T. (1992). *Horace's School: Redesigning the*

American High School. Boston: Houghton Mifflin.

Slavin, R. (1987). Ability grouping and achievement in the elementary school: A best evidence synthesis. *Review of Educational Research, 57,* 293–336.

Slavin, R. (1993.) Ability grouping in the middle grades: Achievement effects and alternatives. *Elementary School Journal, 93,* 535–552.

Starko, A. (1986) *It's about time: Inservice strategies for curriculum compacting.* Mansfield Center, CT: Creative Learning Press.

Stepien, W. J., & Gallagher, S. (developers) (1997). *Problem-based learning across the curriculum.* (An ASCD Professional Inquiry Kit). Alexandria, VA: ASCD.

Sternberg, R. (1985). *Beyond IQ: A triarchic theory of human intelligence.* New York: Cambridge University Press.

Sternberg, R. (1988). *The triarchic mind: A new theory of human intelligence.* New York: Viking.

Sternberg, R. (1997). What does it mean to be smart? *Educational Leadership, 54*(6), 20–24.

Stevenson, C. (1992). *Teaching ten to fourteen year olds.* New York: Longman.

Stevenson, C. (1997). An invitation to join Team 21! In C. Tomlinson (Ed.), *In search of common ground: What constitutes appropriate curriculum and instruction for gifted middle schoolers?* (pp. 31–62). Washington, DC: Curriculum Studies Division of the National Association for Gifted Children.

Stevenson, C., & Carr, J. (Eds.). (1993). *Integrated studies in the middle grades: Dancing through walls.* New York: Teachers College Press.

Strachota, B. (1996). *On their side: Helping children take charge of their learning.* Greenfield, MA: Northeast Foundation for Children.

Sylwester, R. (1995). *A celebration of neurons: An educator's guide to the human brain.* Alexandria, VA: ASCD.

Thomas, L. (1983). *Late night thoughts on listening to Mahler's Ninth Symphony.* New York: Bantam Books.

Tomlinson, C. (1993). Independent study: A flexible tool for encouraging academic and personal growth. *Middle School Journal 25*(1), 55–59.

Tomlinson, C. (1995). Deciding to differentiate instruction in middle school: One school's journey. *Gifted Child Quarterly, 39,* 77–87.

Tomlinson, C. (1995). *How to differentiate instruction in mixed ability classrooms.* Alexandria, VA: ASCD.

Tomlinson, C. (1996). *Differentiating instruction for mixed-ability classrooms* [An ASCD professional inquiry kit]. Alexandria, VA: ASCD.

Tomlinson, C. (1996). Good teaching for one and all: Does gifted education have an instructional identity? *Journal for the Education of the Gifted, 20,* 155–174.

Tomlinson, C. (1997). *Differentiating instruction: Facilitator's guide.* Alexandria, VA: ASCD.

Tomlinson, C., Callahan, C., Moon, T., Tomchin, E., Landrum, M., Imbeau, M., Hunsaker, S., & Eiss, N. (1995). *Preservice teacher preparation in meeting the needs of gifted and other academically diverse students.* Charlottesville, VA: National Research Center on the Gifted and Talented, University of Virginia.

Tomlinson, C., Callahan, C., Tomchin, C., Eiss, N., Imbeau, M., & Landrum, M. (1997). Becoming architects of communities of learning: Addressing academic diversity in contemporary classrooms. *Exceptional Children, 63,* 269–282.

Torp, L., & Sage, S. (1998). *Problems as possibilities: Problem-based learning for K–12 education.* Alexandria, VA: ASCD

Treffinger, D. (1978). Guidelines for encouraging independence and self-direction among gifted students. *Journal of Creative Behavior, 12*(1), 14–20.

Vygotsky, L. (1978). *Mind in society: The development of higher psychological processes* (M. Cole, V. John-Steiner, S. Scribner, & E. Souberman, Eds.). Cambridge, MA: Harvard University Press.

Vygotsky, L. (1986). *Thought and language* (A. Kozulin, Trans. & Ed.). Cambridge, MA: The MIT Press. (Original work published in 1934).

Winebrenner, S. (1992). *Teaching gifted kids in the regular classroom.* Minneapolis, MN: Free Spirit Press.

Index

Page numbers followed by *f* indicates a reference to a figure.

About the Author

Carol Ann Tomlinson is Associate Professor of Educational Leadership, Foundations and Policy at The Curry School of Education, University of Virginia. Tomlinson works with teachers throughout the United States and Canada toward establishing more effectively differentiated classrooms, and is Co-Director of the University of Virginia's Summer Institute on Academic Diversity. She is also Secretary of the Executive Board of the National Association for Gifted Children.

Tomlinson's research interests include differentiated instruction in the middle school, use of multiple intelligences approaches with high-risk and high-potential primary grade learners, and practices of preservice teachers related to academic diversity. She has written many articles, book chapters, and staff development materials that blend classroom and research insights.

Tomlinson's experience includes 21 years as a public school teacher, working with preschoolers, middle school students, and high school students. She has taught English, language arts, German, and history. Tomlinson has administered district-level programs for struggling and advanced learners and was Virginia's Teacher of the Year in 1974.

Carol Ann Tomlinson, Associate Professor of Educational Leadership, Foundations and Policy, Curry School of Education, University of Virginia, Room 179 Ruffner Hall, 405 Emmet St. S., Charlottesville, VA 22903-2494. Phone: (804) 924-7161.